Get

What You

Want

QUENTIN DE LA BEDOYERE

Getting What You Want

PIATKUS

First published in 1994 by
Judy Piatkus (Publishers) Ltd of
5 Windmill Street, London W1P 1HF

The moral right of the author
has been asserted

*A catalogue record for this book is
available from the British Library*

ISBN 0 7499 1418 1 hbk
    0 7499 1423 8 pbk

Edited by Carol Franklin
Designed by Chris Warner

Set in Sabon by Action Typesetting, Gloucester
Printed and bound in Great Britain by
Mackays of Chatham PLC

Contents

What this book is about

This book is about persuasion.

We are all in the business of persuading, or being persuaded, every moment of the day. At home, at work, in our hobbies, dealing with bureaucrats – the game goes on. And there are winners and losers.

Do you want to be a winner? This book will teach you how.

HOW GOOD ARE YOU AT PERSUADING?

Before you start, you may like to test yourself to see just how good you are already at getting your way. Respond to the following questions and statements by ticking (a), (b) or (c).

1. The most effective method of persuasion is through giving rational arguments backed up by reliable evidence.

- ☐ (a) True
- ☑ (b) False
- ☐ (c) True, if the person is intelligent

2. You can become more successful by repeating 'I am successful' several times a day.

■ (a) True
☐ (b) Typical pseudo-science claptrap
☐ (c) True, but only if you're a parrot

3. A friend is starting out on a long motor journey and you want him to be careful. Which would be most effective?

☐ (a) Reminding him of the accident statistics
■ (b) Just telling him to be careful
☐ (c) Telling him a story about an accident you had

4. With all this divorce around, you and your partner are discussing whether to live together before tying the knot. Are couples who do this:

■ (a) More likely to have a stable marriage?
☐ (b) Not affected one way or the other?
☐ (c) Less likely to have a stable marriage?

5. When you go to a selection interview, which is more important:

■ (a) Getting the interviewer to like you?
☐ (b) Showing how well qualified you are for the job?
☐ (c) Being honest and sincere throughout?

6. Children grow up naughty because they aren't sufficiently punished for doing wrong when they are young.

■ (a) True
☐ (b) False
☐ (c) It's all the fault of society

7. To give you the best chance of getting to the top in your business career you should:

☐ (a) Work hard and keep your nose clean
☑ (b) Be a fount of good ideas and be recognised for it
☐ (c) Try and be as like your boss as possible

8. You have a difficult medical or legal problem. Should you:

☑ (a) Consult an expert; they are paid to give you the right advice?
☑ (b) Consult an expert, but take no notice if you disagree?
☐ (c) Make up your own mind without help?

9. You are sitting on a jury deciding the damages to be paid to the claimant. You notice he is a well set-up person, and he vaguely reminds you of a friend of yours. Will the damages you award be:

☐ (a) Likely to be higher as a result?
☐ (b) Lower?
☑ (c) Just the same?

10. Someone gives you an important instruction. She has a standard (BBC) accent. Does this make you:

☑ (a) More likely to respond?
☐ (b) Less likely?
☐ (c) Makes no difference.

Answers

☑ 1. (b)   ☑ 5. (a)   ☑ 8. (b)
☑ 2. (a)   ☒ 6. (b)   ☒ 9. (a)
☒ 3. (c)   ☒ 7. (c)   ☐ 10. (a)
☒ 4. (c)

How did you do? If you scored less than 4, you're really going to need this book just to survive. Given that there are three answers to each question you would expect to score between 3 and 4 just by using a pin. A score between 5 and 8 means that you already have a good grasp in persuasion – and this book will make you a truly formidable opponent in what I like to call 'The Persuasion Game'. If you scored 9 or 10 then you're either brilliant or you cheated. And you'll probably have noticed how I phrased the questions deliberately to put you on the wrong scent. Quizzes or opinion polls can be, and often are, designed to get the answer you want. That's a piece of persuasion in itself!

Don't be discouraged by a low score. I first tried the quiz out on an actuary, a senior personnel manager and two senior secretaries. The highest scorer was a secretary; she got 2. I then spoilt it all by trying it on a marriage counsellor – who got 8.

In a short quiz like this no answer is completely true or completely false. But, as you work your way through the book, you'll find out just why you were right and why you were wrong.

A LIGHTNING OVERVIEW

The book is divided into four sections. Chapters 2 to 5 form Section One – THE BASIC SKILLS. They are concerned with the basic skills every persuader needs. You will use the principles of motivation in Chapter 2 as a starting point for planning your strategy in a variety of persuasion situations. At the end of the chapter you will find a note on action plans for bringing about effective change. In Chapter 3 you will learn the secrets of personal authority and credibility – secrets which will mean that people automatically accept your lead and believe what you say. In Chapter 4 you will discover the unspoken language of persuasion – a language that everyone uses but few understand. In Chapter 5 you will master the techniques of persuasive speaking from the platform.

Section Two, PERSUASION AT WORK, takes us into the world of work. Chapter 6 tells you how to apply for a job and get selected at interview. You may be surprised to discover what really counts in the interviewer's mind – even though they are not aware of it. Once you have your job you will need Chapter 7 to tell you how to plan for the top job and how to use the key skills of management. You won't find this in the usual textbooks.

Section Three, PERSUASION IN THE OUTSIDE WORLD, broadens our horizons. Chapter 8 is a crash commando course in buying, selling and negotiation. You can find out how to beat the professionals at their own game – from the telephone salesperson, to the estate agent, to the supermarket. And, if you're a professional, you'll find a trick or two here that can rocket your sales performance. Chapter 9 tells you how to manage the System – the bureaucrats, the 'experts' and all the other people who use their petty authority to keep us in order.

Section Four, PERSUASION IN THE FAMILY, comprises Chapters 10 and 11, which are about persuasion in long-term relationships – which can include marriage and children. Most persuasion takes place in the context of short-term relationships, so here many of the rules are different. If you want to stay happily married and if you want your children to grow up into constructive, independent adults you'll need to know the rules of the most important Persuasion Game of all.

But start with Chapter 1. This chapter describes the key to persuasion – the strange ways in which the human mind works. Throughout millions of years of evolution our minds have developed ways of making judgements. Most of these were useful once and some still are. But because they are automatic they give the persuasion player great power to influence just what conclusion your opponents will come to. And your opponents, unless they are skilled players too, will never know what has happened.

MAKING THE BEST USE OF THIS BOOK

There is a great deal of information in this book. How are you going to master it? You can make use of a simple technique which is based on how the brain understands and remembers new information. We learn better and quicker if we have seen the whole picture first, and then turn to the details. If you start with the details you will have no larger framework in which to store them and no way of seeing how to put them together. Your brain will blow a fuse. So try this method, which you will also find useful for other learning situations.

- Read through the list of chapter titles, then flip though the book just glancing at the section headings, the lists of reminders, strategies and tips. By the time you've done that you'll already have a good idea of what the book is about.
- In Chapter 12 you'll find a list of 'programs' – my name for the automatic ways in which the brain makes judgements. Read it through quickly, but don't study it at this stage. There is an Index of Programs at the end of the book.
- Now read through the book. Don't stop for particular items, other than the quizzes, but mark – perhaps with a soft pencil in the margin – any sections or ideas which particularly interest you, or skills you would particularly like to master.
- Then take one item. Perhaps because it is immediately relevant like applying for a new job or preparing a speech – or perhaps because it's a skill that interests you and you really believe you can grasp it quickly. Devise an action plan for this item. Really making an improvement here will give you the confidence to move on to other ideas. If you try to master the whole book at once, you will certainly fail.
- At the end of Chapter 2 you will find the outline of an action plan. You will need to adapt it to fit in with each set of circumstances, but the basic principles are here.

● The main point to remember is that persuasion is a *skill*; it can only be mastered with practice. You can read as many books on juggling as you like, but you won't become a juggler until you've practised. Both in the text and in the strategy lists you will find tips and ideas for practice. But they are only a starting point – you will have to modify them to suit your own personality and needs.

Good luck and good persuading!

The masculine gender is used generally throughout the book simply for convenience. The points made apply equally to both sexes – except where the context makes it clear that the reference is to a specific sex.

1
The persuadable brain

WE ALL HAVE THE POWER of rational thought, but we use it rarely. Most of our decisions are made through a series of automatic brain 'programs'. By understanding and invoking these programs we can gain real persuasion power. But we must also learn to recognise and resist the persuasion programs that may influence us.

How GOOD ARE YOU at estimating heights? Before you answer that question you may like to consider the strange case of the speaker who grew by two-and-a-half inches before the eyes of his audiences.

After the applause had died away and the speaker had left the room, the students were asked to estimate his height. He went to the next class to give his lecture, and the next. In all, five classes estimated his height – and they disagreed: each class added half an inch to the estimate until, by the fifth class, he was thought to be two-and-a-half inches taller than when he had started.

The answer didn't lie in built-up shoes, but in the importance of the speaker. To the first class he was introduced as a student from Cambridge, to the second he was introduced as a demonstrator – and so on through the academic ranks until, when introduced as a professor, he reached his full stature.

So it seems that there is a little program in the human brain which says: tall people are important, so the more important a person is the taller they must be.

Of course the audiences in that story were only making a casual judgement; one would expect much more accuracy when the decision really mattered — when someone's career and liberty depended on making the right decision, for instance. If you were a member of a jury would you be influenced by whether the accused was attractive or not? Unthinkable? In that case, you're an exception. Attractive defendants are twice as likely to be found not guilty by juries as unattractive defendants.

That looks like another little program in the brain: attractive people are likely to be innocent; unattractive people are likely to be guilty.

> *The effects of attractiveness are present at an early age. Unattractive children are more likely to be blamed for naughtiness than attractive ones — both by adults and other children.*

In front of you is a man answering 20 questions in mental arithmetic. He makes just 5 mistakes. Do you judge him to be good or poor at mental arithmetic? The answer is — it depends on where the mistakes come. If they mostly come in the first half of the questions you are likely to judge him as poor; if they come in the second half you are likely to judge him as good. The reason for that is another program in the brain which not only makes first impressions very important, but which also makes us stay with those impressions, ignoring any later evidence which seems to be contradictory. So, if your first impression is that he's poor at mental arithmetic, even getting the rest of the questions right is unlikely to change your mind. And vice versa.

In an experiment a number of student classes were told about the new lecturer who would visit them shortly. The introducer mentioned some good and some less good characteristics of the lecturer. Although the same words were always used, the order varied. After each lecture the students were asked to rate the lecturer's performance. They rated him more highly if the good characteristics had been mentioned before rather than after the less good characteristics.

THE PERSUADER AND THE PROGRAM

The human brain contains dozens of little programs just like the ones I have just described. Some of them are personal to us. That is, we have built them through our own life experiences, but others we seem to have inherited. You could think of them as convenient short cuts; instead of thinking, which is hard work and takes time, we switch on an automatic program which does our thinking for us. (Note: I have chosen the transatlantic spelling for the word program because I am using it in the same sense as a computer program. That is, a sequence of instructions which is triggered by an initial command or stimulus.)

These programs are normally rather useful to us, although it's easy to see how they could mislead – as the examples have shown. But they are always useful to skilled persuaders because their knowledge of the programs in other people's minds enables them to make moves in the persuasion game which lead to success.

Philippa is an attractive woman in her 50s. Her car broke down on a parking meter and although she left a note she was given a ticket. She was sufficiently irritated to challenge the decision in the local court. She made up carefully and chose her clothes to give the impression of elegant respectability. Controlling her sense of righteous indignation (to which she is prone under normal circumstances), she turned on the charm. By the time she had explained how helpless she had felt in the face of mechanical breakdown and how sad it was that her husband hadn't been at home to help her, the magistrate was practically holding her hand in sympathy. The case was dismissed without further ado.

It may be worth mentioning – in case she reads this – that Philippa is one of the least helpless people I know. She had decided to combine a number of programs in order to win her case: appearance (clothes are one of the most immediate ways in which we judge people); attractiveness (both in her looks and in her manner); and vulnerability (often a winner when a masculine mind has to be suborned). If the magistrate had been a woman she would only have had to adapt her story a little to focus on the disadvantages women suffer when faced by the male preserve of the motor car engine.

LIGHTNING REMINDER

★ *We have automatic reactions to certain stimuli like attractiveness or height. These are called programs.*

★ *If you think you are not susceptible to programs you are probably wrong, if only because you don't realise that you are.*

PLAYING THE PERSUASION GAME

Dr Eric Berne in his classic *Games People Play* defines a game as 'an ongoing series of complementary ulterior transactions leading to a well-defined, predictable outcome'. Persuasion is a game for two or more players – although there is a solo version called auto-persuasion. The object of the game is to induce the other player to think or to act in the way that you have chosen. A successful player uses a variety of moves and counter-moves which are based on the way they believe their opponent will react to their communication. The moves have been developed from observing how the human mind characteristically processes information. While all players take part, since the habit of making persuasion moves is in-built, some or all players in any given match may not be aware that they are playing. This can be a disadvantage for them.

Being a game, persuasion is normally enjoyable. There are few activities which give more pleasure than taking part in a match between skilled players. However – as in other games – the need to win can obscure the enjoyment. This is more likely to be the case when the stakes are high. Philippa enjoyed herself because she was playing for relatively low stakes. Had she been playing to retain her job or to negotiate a major financial deal it might have been different. But, all other things being equal, the player who can continue to maintain a high level of enjoyment, irrespective of the stakes, will play the better game. Anxiety is not a good ally.

The Machiavellian intelligence hypothesis is the impressive name given to a respectable theory which seeks to explain why the human brain has developed, through evolution, to levels of sophistication far in advance of those required to be an efficient hunter-gatherer. The hypothesis is that successful human beings were those who were genetically best fitted for the need to get a good bargain, to induce others to do their will, to control their social environment. Through these skills they achieved a higher standard of living, bred more and reared more of their young to maturity.

If this theory is true it follows that the persuasion game (although played at a lower level, and presumably unconsciously, by some animal species) is a fundamental human activity, expressing and developing the range of human mental capacity. And it is well named; Machiavelli's *Prince* is a basic text for serious players.

LIGHTNING REMINDER

★ **The persuasion game is won by those who understand and use the ways that the human brain makes judgements.**

★ **Human progress owes much to our need to play the persuasion game well.**

BUILDING PROGRAMS

The programs described above provide examples from which the player can derive effective moves. In the course of this book we will look at these and other programs as they might be used in practical circumstances. Later in this chapter we will look at other aspects of the brain's methods of processing which are useful to the persuader. But first we need to understand how programs come about. One major source of programs is our experience of life which continually builds, shapes and modifies the programs in our minds.

A good example of this is stereotyping.

The stereotype program

Think for a moment about the categories below:

● men with long hair

- women who wear heavy make-up
- accountants

Each of these categories tends to suggest a number of associated characteristics – sometimes good and sometimes bad. For instance you might instinctively think of men with long hair as being rather creative, interesting and attractive; or you might think of them as unreliable, pushy layabouts. That could depend on who you are, and what your previous experience of long-haired men has been.

Everyone uses such stereotypes for short-cut judgements. When we meet an accountant we don't attempt immediately to analyse character, we make a number of assumptions about likely behaviour based on our stereotype. As we get to know an accountant better we notice the differences between the behaviour and the stereotype, and modify our judgement. But the stereotype is the starting point. By the way, when you read the word 'accountant', did you think of a male or a female? Perhaps there's a stereotype working there, too.

We are right in calling the stereotyping program prejudice – because prejudgement is what the word means. But in fact we have little choice. Life moves so quickly that unless we have a set of assumptions about different sorts of people ready to hand we would have no starting point from which to make any decisions at all.

The skilled persuader uses stereotyping as an effective move, applicable to a wide range of circumstances:

Released from a long day of high level board meetings a senior executive allowed joie de vivre rather than prudence to dictate his speed on the long dual carriageway. Soon a flashing light and a police siren told him he had overdone it. Spotting from his expression that the police officer had marked him down as a motorcycle tearaway, he pulled in to the side and, as quickly as possible, removed his crash helmet. He could see the policeman's expression change as he revealed a middle aged, bespectacled head. The policeman

|| *instantaneously switched stereotypes, and the courteous* || *ticking off he gave left them both the best of friends.*

Even the skilled persuader is susceptible to stereotypes. However, by developing awarenesss of your own susceptibility you have a good chance of preventing your stereotypes from hardening. Review them frequently and always be ready to modify them in the light of experience.

Language programs

We have just seen an example of a language program through two words, prejudice and prejudgement. At a literal level both words mean the same thing, but they carry quite different emotional messages. No wonder that the persuader is concerned to choose words with care to ensure that the message has the right impact. Compare the following descriptions:

'I didn't like the little dictator who ran the meeting. He had one of those toothbrush moustaches, and he sat up so straight you'd think he had a broom handle up his back. You could see he'd spent his life ordering people about, and the committee were certainly going to knuckle under. Every time I made a remark he fixed me with an accusing eye, daring me to disagree with one of his pet ideas.'

'Thank heavens we had a firm chairman. He was a neat looking man with a military bearing. And that showed in the way he controlled the meeting. He'd obviously done some thinking about the problem and if you got off the point, as I did occasionally, he'd just give me a little private glance, as though to remind me that we had business to be done.'

It seems that we learn to use the power of words quite early. The three-year-old who says 'I need an ice-cream' instead of 'I want an ice-cream' is already well on the way to becoming a skilled persuader.

High level players mount their first line of defence by mentally translating the words they hear in order to detect the attitude of the speaker. One effective counter-ploy is the challenge:

Naïve enquirer: *What you're talking about is manipulating people.*

Author: *Do you know the origin of the word manipulation?*

Naïve enquirer: *Er, it's from the Latin I suppose.*

Author: *Yes, it comes from the word* manus – *which means hand. Manipulation and handling mean exactly the same thing. Personally I prefer to use the neutral word – it's less manipulative.*

Think about the following:

- If you were attacking fox hunting, what stereotype would you use?
- If you were attacking hunt saboteurs, how might you use the language program?

INHERITING PROGRAMS

In practice the distinction between programs that are built and programs that are inherited is not clear cut. For example, the ability to smile is inherited; it occurs in all cultures at about the same age. But the baby learns very quickly how it can use a smile to get desirable attention from adults. Later on its parents will teach it to reinforce the smile by using 'please' and 'thank you' – thus incorporating another automatic program. This program says: I will be more inclined to agree to a request if I feel I could refuse it if I wanted to. Of course saying 'please' is so nominal in our culture that its real meaning has virtually disappeared. But our programmed brain still reacts to the word – or, rather, reacts negatively if the word is missing.

> *Hamlet said, '. . . one may smile and smile and be a villain'. Smiling is not always enough, as one civil service report established – smiling is no substitute for 'conformance to customer expectations'. But it's a good start.*

All gazelles together

For a good example of an inherited program, think of a wildlife series on television. The herd of gazelles are grazing peacefully on the open plain when suddenly a predator appears. The whole herd moves as one. And for a very good reason – the predator will catch any straggler or any animal that it can separate from the herd. Not surprisingly, gazelles have inherited a strong herding instinct because any ancestor without that instinct in its genes did not survive long enough to bear young.

It is reasonable to suppose that, somewhere along the evolutionary line that led to human beings, our own ancestors learnt that running with the herd in conditions of danger and uncertainty was a good survival strategy. And it still is today. Suppose you meet a group of people running towards you shouting 'Fire!' You would be unwise not to join them. But, like so many of the instincts formed under quite different conditions, it can often prove inappropriate or dangerous.

The popular music industry largely survives on the herd instinct. If the promoters can get a new recording played sufficiently often, its popularity will grow almost irrespective of its merit. After all, everyone else likes it, so I must, too. Fashion obeys the same rules. I suspect that if green lipstick were mentioned as being the 'in' shade in a few key magazines, it would soon be a common sight in the high street. Exaggerated? Look at some of the fashions which have succeeded in our own time – let alone in history.

The herd program is extremely powerful. Many people disagree with the publication of opinion polls in the period before an election and some countries ban them. There is a well-based fear that people will decide their vote according to others' intentions and thus distort the democratic process.

The herd program is the basis of many successful moves in the persuasion game. Politicians have it at their fingertips. For example they will often defend a controversial new measure like compulsory seat belts or universal identity cards by pointing out that country X or country Y already has this measure working successfully. The context in which country X is operating this measure – such as other regulations, different demographics or different traditions – is not mentioned. And we, the listeners, find ourselves thinking that if X and Y find it works we will too.

The business persuader finds the herd program useful. One successful salesman asks his best customers to write him a commendation on their headed paper. At an appropriate point in the sales interview he will produce these letters for his prospective customer to read. He has as many available as is required to convince the new customer not only that they will be safe in taking the salesman's advice, but that they might even be left dangerously out on a limb if they fail to do so.

Children are natural herders. How often have you been subjected to the appeal that some new toy must be provided or bed time extended on the grounds that simply everyone else in the class enjoys these benefits? Either we comply to save the little mite from ostracism or we wisely point out the foolishness of being like the rest of the herd – conveniently forgetting that many of our own decisions are made on just the same basis.

While using the herd program effectively the good persuader will always remember Sydney Smith's dictum that 'Minorities are almost always in the right'. He believed that herds are essentially mindless and cannot therefore be a good guide for the rational person. Think of Rothschild's investment advice 'Buy when everyone else is selling, and sell when everyone else is buying' and extend this principle into your general affairs.

But do not forget that minorities are only 'almost always' in the right – especially when you meet a crowd shouting 'Fire!'

LIGHTNING REMINDER

- ★ *Programs can be inherited (perhaps through evolution) or cultivated – often both.*

- ★ *Remember the powerful herd instinct. Can you remember the last time you allowed it to persuade you?*

THE MASTER PROGRAM

In looking at programs, we have sampled useful tactical moves and throughout the book other programs will be introduced in their practical context. The process involves the brain taking the new information and selecting an appropriate program against which to judge it. Thus, faced with a 'university professor', the 'important people are tall' program snaps into action. Seeing everyone buying product X calls up the 'running with the herd is safe' program.

This demonstrates a master program which lies behind the art of getting what you want. This master program instructs the brain to make its judgements by comparing new information with the programs or information which is already present. Judgement is always relative. And since the brain does not use the whole of the information which is at its disposal, but only that part which it thinks is relevant, the fundamental strategy is to ensure that you control the information or the program against which the judgement is being made.

> *The story is told about two monks – Brother James and Brother John – who were both heavy smokers. The rules of their Order obliged them to say lengthy prayers*

in their cells during each day; this was hard for them because, by about the third psalm, they began to suffer from tobacco deprivation. So they decided to put their problem to their abbot. When they next met, Brother James was looking rather depressed. Brother John, who was looking rather cheerful, asked him how he had got on. 'Terrible,' said James. 'I asked the abbot if I could smoke while I was praying, and he gave me a real ticking off and three extra penances for even daring to put the question. How did you get on?'

'No problem at all,' said Brother John. 'I asked him if I could pray while I was smoking. He congratulated me on my piety, and said I was one of the best monks in the monastery.'

You may like to reflect on why Brother John was successful and why Brother James failed. After all they both made the same request.

The comparing brain

The human brain is faced by an enormous task. It has to process a great deal of information – often at lightning speed, so it devises short cuts which help it to reduce processing time. The master program of working through comparisons enables the brain to confine itself to looking at the differences, or the similarities, between the new information it receives and the old information which is already present.

So the brain has evolved to become very good at recognising and judging differences – particularly those which are important to it. We can see this most directly in the physical channels which convey information to the brain – the senses and the nervous system. For example, ask yourself these questions.

- Why do we often fail to observe objects until they move?
- Why do we not hear a ticking clock, although it may sound quite loud when our attention is drawn to it?

- Why have people become, in recent years, very sensitive to the smell of tobacco smoke?
- Why, if we place our left and right hands in bowls of hot and cold water respectively, does a bowl of tepid water feel cold to the left hand and warm to the right hand?

The answer to all these questions is, of course, that the nervous system is tuned to observe differences. Thus the visual system has special receptors which are activated by movement; these are much more sensitive in animals like cats. The brain has filtered out the ticking clock because it has habituated itself to the sound and judged it as unimportant – leaving the auditory system clear to notice more significant noises. Non smokers notice tobacco smoke because there are far more smoke-free environments today. The left hand has become accustomed to warmth through being in the hot water; the new information from the bowl of tepid water is interpreted as cold by contrast.

The value of noticing differences is clear. They are the first sign of danger and also the first sign of opportunity for food. If raw survival is the imperative then a species needs to develop such a mechanism rather quickly before it ceases to be a species altogether. But the senses and the nervous system are really extensions of the brain, and the strategy of working by comparisons operates at all levels.

Are people in general happier than they were, say, two or three hundred years ago? Of course they should be. Most people in our society have warm houses and ample food, with access to anaesthetics and television. Many diseases have been eradicated, and infant and maternal deaths are rare. If these benefits were suddenly withdrawn we would be deeply unhappy – making conscious comparisons of how our state had changed. But the literature of earlier times does not show that people were more or less happy than they are today. In the rather superficial sense in which I am using the word, our scale of happiness can be defined as the difference between our expectations and our experience. Our feelings depend on the comparison.

An important program which stems from our readiness to

notice differences is called 'prominence'. It tells us that information which is in the forefront of our mind – perhaps because of a recent dramatic incident – is of greater importance than the facts necessarily warrant. For example, we tend to drive more carefully if we have just witnessed a serious road accident, or we overestimate the incidence of a crime if we have recently encountered it.

We also meet it in less dramatic ways and the skilled persuader will often find the means of ensuring that the right incident is in the forefront of the mind they want to persuade. Or, knowing what is in the forefront of the person's mind, the skilled persuader will present the ideas in a form which relates to it. You will encounter this technique again in this book. It was once said of the managing director of an international company: 'The two most influential people in this organisation are the managing director and the person he last spoke to.'

> *Our comparisons are frequently contaminated by the prominence program. Fairground rides may seem to be dangerous because accidents get publicity, yet cycling on a main road or driving a car (for the same length of time) are several times more dangerous according to statistics from the Health and Safety Executive.*

Personnel officers know this. We would all like to be paid as much as possible, but what really causes a storm is differences in pay which appear to be unfair. Why should Robinson get £5,000 a year more than me when his work is no harder and his responsibility actually less? The comparison counts more than the absolute amount. This was illustrated by an occasion when a group of workers settled for a lower wage which kept them ahead of an 'inferior' group – rather than a higher wage which nevertheless lost them their 'superior' differential. Trade unions have a history of leapfrogging: if Ford workers are getting a 10 per cent rise, that's what my union should be demanding too, and perhaps a little bit more. No wonder personnel officers try to avoid publishing individuals' salaries and develop complex systems of establishing pay grades by means of apparently objective measurement.

THE SKILLED PERSUADER AND THE BRAIN'S COMPARISONS

Looking at some ways in which the skilled persuader uses comparisons will illustrate how they work in a number of circumstances. The persuader uses two methods: one is by deliberately planting the information against which the comparison is made; the other is by hitchhiking on information which is already present. In practice the two approaches are often hard to distinguish and are frequently used together.

Since the brain does not make its comparisons by recalling its complete store of information but only the segment of information it thinks relevant, your task as a persuader is to guide the opponent's brain towards selecting the particular frame of reference you need for your purpose.

Planting the information

The story of how Brother John obtained permission to smoke by the way he made his request provided a good example of planting the information through which a different comparison – and therefore a different judgement – was made. But some further examples will show other ways in which the games player can use this move.

Take, for instance, the expense versus the investment categories. You are considering the purchase of a set of encyclopedias which will cost several hundred pounds. Looked at within an expense category you might well be comparing the cost with the items which you have to forgo in order to buy the set. But the salesperson asks you to think about what the encyclopedias will do for your children's education. Would not the books be an investment in your children's future, yielding returns in benefit to them far greater than the present cost? The frame of reference has been changed, and your decision may too.

In a similar vein, you might be considering whether to take out a pension scheme. You are earning £20,000 a year and the pensions salesperson, who has not read this book, suggests that you put £2,000 a year into a retirement scheme. It's a large sum of money, and you refuse. A year later, having read this book, he visits you again. This time he reminds you that you have 30 years to go before retirement and that you might reasonably expect to live for 15 years on your pension. That's two years' earning for each year of retirement. He suggests that you should put no more than 10 per cent of your income into your retirement fund. The second suggestion sounds, if anything, rather cheap. Why?

A related way of getting the information to be used into the required category is the use of analogy.

First player	*I see there's an exhibition of Kandinsky this week.*
Second player	*Kandinsky? He's that abstract painter isn't he? I think abstract painting's just a con. It doesn't represent anything, it doesn't mean anything; it's just painted shapes.*
First player	*I thought you were a music lover.*
Second player	*So?*
First player	*What does Bach represent? What does he mean?*
Second player	*He doesn't have to mean anything; he's just a feast for the ears.*
First player	*For the trained ear, perhaps. Think of Kandinsky as a feast for the trained eye.*

That, by the way, was Kandinsky's own analogy; he wrote in 1912 that he was attempting to express the artist's soul through vision as the musician does through sound. As another example, imagine a managing director explaining to the board why he is recommending a tough cut-back in the business, together with many redundancies. He might explain that, like the good gardener, he was pruning back the weak shoots so that the full strength of the company could be channelled into strong new growth. The analogy turns an unwelcome business decision into an exercise in good husbandry.

This analogy might be less helpful in the actual interview when a faithful company employee is being told that his services are no longer required. The comparison with weak shoots could be tactless. An alternative method here is to change the frame of reference by asking the employee to look at the situation from another's point of view. You might put it to the employee like this: 'Joe, I can see how tough this is on you. But imagine you were sitting on my side of the desk. Here is someone who's a fine worker, but the job simply doesn't exist any longer. What would *you* do in my position?'

Hitchhiking on existing information

You are sitting in a train in a station. You become aware that the train is starting to move forward very smoothly. But is it your train or just the train at the adjacent platform moving off in the opposite direction?

The road engineer uses this built-in program of the relativity of movement in order to persuade us to slow down for roundabouts. He paints yellow bars on the road in the throat of the roundabout, but each successive bar is closer to the one before. Since we automatically judge our speed by the passing of the bars (the eye is constructed to pay attention to bars and edges), we are fooled into overestimating our speed, so that we brake in good time. This is a benign persuasion move, but a persuasion move none the less.

The herd instinct, the obedience instinct and the first impression instinct have already given us examples of the deeper psychological programs on which the persuasion player can hitch a ride. In later chapters we will meet them again. Another example is reciprocation; it has many uses.

There is a deep laid program which tells us that gifts have to be reciprocated. In some societies this is very explicit: the level and the type of reciprocal gift may be laid down by social convention, and failure to conform is a serious gaffe. In Western society reciprocation is less structured although, even here, there is broad agreement about the type of gift that one might bring to, say, a dinner party. Among the franker classes of our society a phrase like 'I owe you one' is an explicit acknowledgement that one favour requires another in return.

In business, gifts are common − from the glossy calendar to a day on a grouse moor. But the effect of such gifts is blunted by the knowledge that the cost has come out of the company pocket. A personal gift (which may well take the form of a favour or a service rather than an object) can be more powerful. And although there may be a rough matching in the size of the gifts, in some instances it is the actual giving of the gift which has the effect.

A neighbour of mine had a young lodger who seemed to be unable to keep her room tidy. Just as my neighbour was preparing to give her notice, the lodger wrote her a little letter saying: 'I just wanted you to know how happy I am living in your lovely house.' That was many months ago, and the lodger is still there − and her room is still untidy.

An interesting case of reciprocation is given by Robert Cialdini, in *Influence, Science and Practice,* of the members of the Hare Krishna society who would beg for funds in public places such as airports. Their campaign was not successful until they adopted the strategy of giving a flower to the passers-by. The flower itself was a trivial gift (indeed swiftly discarded flowers could be recovered from litter bins for re-use), but the effect on contributions was dramatic. Once the gift had been accepted it became psychologically difficult not to make a return.

A skilful persuader may adopt the habit of looking for opportunities to make gifts or provide little services, confident that a return will be made whenever it should be needed. Or the gift may be related to a specific request you are planning to make, being careful to avoid giving the impression that the two elements of the transaction were intended to be connected.

PERSONAL PROGRAMS

While these programs are common to human nature they affect individuals in different ways and with different force. For instance the herd instinct may be ineffective against an opponent who is naturally independent or has built up defences. So the persuasion player will alter his or her strategy and choose the programs to use as a result of observing the individual character. Many of these will be personal to the player's opponent.

A good motor car salesperson will often start by enquiring after a potential customer's existing model, and asking how they liked it. From the answer the salesperson will learn whether the customer values performance, comfort or gadgetry. When demonstrating possible new models the salesperson will stress the way in which they meet the customer's interests, following the old dictum 'find out what a person wants, then show them how to get it'.

Marianne is a middle-ranking executive who is much preoccupied by making sure that her gender does not hold her back. Demonstrate to her how a particular job will enable her to show her paces against her masculine peers and she will grab at it.

Charlie grew up in a poor background and is very careful about money. You can persuade him to do almost anything provided you show him that he is getting a bargain.

Fred had a henpecked father. He now believes that husbands should make all family decisions. And so he does. But all his decisions are really Mrs Fred's – who knows a thing or two about the persuasion game.

THE MANUAL OVERRIDE

The power of programs might lead us to think that human beings are irrational creatures capable of being moulded like putty into the shape chosen by the persuader. It's a depressing picture. But not a complete one.

Think of the modern camera. It will have automatic devices for focusing and selecting the right shutter speed for different conditions. For most photographs, most of the time, all you have to do is point and shoot – the camera will get it right. The programs in the brain and the strategy of judging by comparisons perform a similar function – they are quick, convenient and save trouble. Most of the time they get it right, although some of the programs which were incorporated a very long time ago can give unexpected results.

But photographers can choose to override the automatic mechanisms and choose their own settings. The brain is just the same. We can defend ourselves against the programs and choose our own settings.

If you know that you have a program which tells you that attractive people are virtuous, you can make allowances for that – and concentrate on other evidence. If you know that you are subject to the herd instinct you may hear the warning bell which reminds you that the herd is a poor guide. If someone presents you with a gift you can fight the instinct to reciprocate and consider whether you are being subjected to gentle bribery. If someone challenges you with an appealing analogy you can test it to see whether it really applies. (For instance, did you consider whether the analogy between the brain and an automatic camera was a valid one or did you accept it at face value?)

Your first line of defence should be your understanding of how judgements are made. In theory, at least, a skilled player of the persuasion game ought to be in a strong position. But this is not always so. Life comes at all of us so quickly that we often realise too late that we have walked into another fool's mate. I still find that an item advertised at £499 seems cheaper than one at £500. I still warm to attractive people even though I know this is no guide to character. I still find it easier to go with the crowd because going against it is uncomfortable and frightening.

In general, people are less likely to be victims of their own brain programs if the topic is one of deep interest and importance to them. It motivates them towards a more cautious analysis which requires them to replace their automatic response with their intelligence. As we will see in looking at persuasion in marriage (Chapter 10), persuasion strategies need to be modified to take into account the long-term relationships in which the effectiveness of any persuasion move is tested through experience and the passage of time.

But most persuasion games are about everyday matters in which the opponent is not so deeply engaged or which take place over short periods of time. The issue will be lost or won through the skill of the player who commands the sort of moves I have described in this chapter. As we progress through different practical situations in this book, you will see some of the examples being put to use in a variety of different circumstances and you will learn new patterns, new programs and new moves in the fascinating game of persuasion.

LIGHTNING REMINDER

★ *Study the personal programs of your opponents and use them.*

★ *The 'manual override' is a good defence against programs, but even the skilled persuaders can be caught out if they are not careful.*

STRATEGIES FOR THE PERSUASION GAME

At this stage we have only looked at persuasion in a very general way; we will be seeing how the techniques are used in later chapters of the book.

- Start looking out in yourself and others for instances of programs in action.
- If you can't find any in yourself, decide whether you are unnaturally rational or just a sucker.
- The next time you realise that a program is influencing your judgement, stop! Think! Apply the manual override.

SECTION ONE

The basic skills

2
Auto-persuasion and motivation

THROUGH UNDERSTANDING how we are motivated we can learn how to motivate others. The motivation triangle of purpose, price and probability is the key to this. The limited image performance syndrome (LIPS) is a major factor in motivation – and we can choose just how unlimited to be!

THERE IS A DIFFERENCE between persuading people to change their minds and persuading them to change their actions. Agreement is not the same as motivation. We meet the difference every day within ourselves whenever we accept that we ought to do something or that it would benefit us to do something – and yet we fail to do it.

This chapter is about motivation: the principles that will guide us in motivating ourselves and in motivating others.

Our internal worlds are full of the things we would like to be or do. As a child you might have wanted to fly an aeroplane or win at Wimbledon. As you grew older your wants may have developed – to have a happy marriage, to hold down an important job, to write an immortal novel. By now you may have achieved some of these wants and some may be yet to come. But the key to our success lies in how well we can motivate ourselves. We must learn to play and win the auto-persuasion game. In doing so, we will learn a great deal about motivating others.

Look at the motivation triangle below. It reminds us that in order to be motivated to action three conditions have to be fulfilled.

- **Purpose**   We have to *want* to achieve something in order to consider it in the first place.
- **Price**   There will be a price, in effort or sacrifice or in some other way, which we will need to pay if we are to achieve the objective. Notice there is a balance here – the more we want something the higher the price we will be ready to pay. We will only act if the price seems worth it.
- **Probability**   We may want something and the 'price' may be right, but we still won't act unless we believe that our action has a good enough probability of being successful in obtaining our purpose. There is a balance here, too. The more we want something or the lower the price we have to pay, the more we will be willing to give it a try.

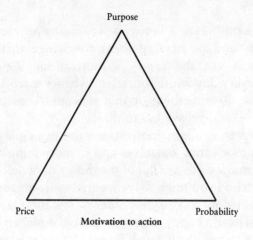

Motivation to action

> *'Do you sincerely want to be rich?' was a question which Bernard Cornfeld put to his salespeople in the 1960s. The fact that he ended up in jail is beside the point, his psychology was right. If you sincerely want to be rich, then you'll pay a high price. And Cornfeld showed his salespeople how to do it, and gave them the confidence to succeed.*

But whether our Purpose is to become rich, or to become powerful, or just to read *War and Peace,* our assessment of the Motivation Triangle will dictate what we actually do, not just what we think we should do.

PURPOSE

Purpose, at first sight, looks straightforward enough. After all, we know what we want out of life and what we don't want. But things are not always what they seem.

> *Marriage counsellors find it important to help clients discover their real objectives. Initially it can seem quite clear: 'I want my husband to stop beating me up' or 'I want my wife to be faithful'. But as the interviews progress the true objective begins to emerge. It might turn out to be 'I want to have more control over my life' or 'I want to be sexually self-confident'. It is only when counsellor and client discover the true objective that serious work can begin. The initial objective is sincere; it comes from the need to solve the immediate problem. But it may turn out to be a symptom of an underlying objective. By the time this has been dealt with, the symptom will have disappeared.*

Purposes often turn out to be mixed. A friend of mine wants to write an immortal novel because he wants to live for ever. He

told me that he could visualise someone in a hundred years'
time picking a battered volume out of a junk bookshop, and
finding that he could still communicate with them. He has a
personal program which tells him that novels are the only form
of creativity which really counts.

> *Gary was a top salesman, paid on commission. He*
> *earned a very large income and every year he set out to*
> *achieve a new record in his level of sales.*
>
> *Since he lived in the same small house and appeared to*
> *have a modest standard of living, people wondered why*
> *he bothered to urge himself onwards. But the reason was*
> *simple. His personal programs indicated to him that*
> *people were measured by what they earned. And*
> *everyone knew what Gary earned because he told them.*
> *Each step up in his income was a step up in his self-*
> *esteem. Each new record made him more of a man.*

Do you want to read *War and Peace* in order to benefit from
Tolstoy's description of human affairs or because you want to
be able to say that you've read it?

Because our Purposes are often unrecognised, and sometimes
mixed, they can be hard to detect. But it's important to be clear
what they are – whether you are dealing with your own
motivation or motivating another. Mistake the purpose and
you may find perseverance hard, because the first small
successes do not give the satisfaction expected. The overt need
is being fulfilled but the covert need, the hidden agenda, may be
untouched.

The hidden agenda

J. Pierpont Morgan, the American banker, said: 'A man
generally has two reasons for doing a thing; one that sounds
good and a *real* one.' You need to know your own hidden
agenda and your opponent's hidden agenda. The following list,
in which the hidden agenda is shown in bold italics, is not
entirely serious but it will demonstrate what I mean.

'I think a person should put something back into society, that's why I contribute to charities and sit on charity committees.'

I want a knighthood.

'I am sitting quietly during this meeting because it's a serious subject and I want to give a considered view after I've heard all the arguments.'

I don't know what they're talking about and if I open my mouth I'll make a fool of myself.

'I am being nice to Mrs Jones because I believe that colleagues need to work as a team, even if they don't see eye to eye.'

I loathe the woman, but if I'm nice to her she'll find it hard to be nasty to me.

'I will always defend the freedom of the press against censorship; people have the right to know the truth.'

Without sex scandals how do we increase circulation?

'Darling, I'm not going to buy you a mountain bike for Christmas, they're far too dangerous.'

Mountain bikes are expensive.

'In this company we always put customers first.'

The more important they feel, the more they'll spend.

'I'm reading this book to increase my effectiveness in my home and in my job.'

I'm reading this book because I'd rather have an edge over other people than let them get an edge over me.

This list is almost certainly too cynical, and in truth we are usually a mixture of worthy and less worthy motives. But you need to know which way your opponent is really pointing if you want to hitch a ride to your chosen destination.

LIGHTNING REMINDER

★ *To motivate remember the balance between purpose, price and probability.*

★ *Only the real purpose motivates. Find out what it is.*

PRICE

The Price we are prepared to pay in order to achieve our purpose can be in different currencies: it can be in cash, it can be in time, it can be in health, it can be in the sacrifice of personal relationships – and many other forms. The weighing of the balance is often delicate and is often more dependent on our personal programs than on strict logic.

What would you pay for a restored Vincent Black Shadow motorcycle? Most people, I suspect, would pay very little. But a vintage motorcycle buff might pay a great deal – even though, in every measurable respect, it is inferior to a modern machine at a fraction of the price. Suppose, however, it would fulfil a childhood dream – how do you put a price on that?

Of course the bike enthusiast could think of a rational justification: a Black Shadow could be an excellent investment. And the enthusiast would prefer not to think about the fact that to rely on it as an investment would mean endless cleaning and maintenance, and probably very little usage.

I have a friend who is in a dilemma. He has been offered a job in the United States which not only increases his salary substantially, but would be a shrewd long-term career move. His problem is that he has two children who are in the course of preparing for public examinations. Initially he discounted the offer; his children's education was inviolable. But recently he has begun to wonder whether the advantages he will gain might not eventually benefit the children. They will get a broader experience of life, and his improved financial position might even enable him to give them a better start in life. Besides, it cannot be good for the children to have a father who might resent them for holding him back in his career. I think another week will be enough to decide him. By restating the price to himself in acceptable terms it will become affordable, and he will go.

Psychological accounting

Decisions like these are painful to make because a loss (Price) has to be measured against the gain (Purpose). Fortunately human beings have programs which enable them to deaden pain. For instance, at the physiological level even chronic pain can become bearable as the receptors in the brain accustom themselves and become less sensitive. In this case, however, the pain is psychological and the deadening program is called psychological accounting.

Psychological accounting lessens the pain and increases the profit. In the examples above the process of rationalising Price has already started. But it will continue, even after the decision has been irrevocably made.

Typically, there are two stages. The first is regret. We wonder whether we have made a terrible mistake in buying that very expensive hi-fi equipment. We may even toy with the idea of searching for a flaw and insisting that the shop takes it back. But once we are resigned to the purchase the psychological accounting begins. This can be tackled from both ends. After all the price wasn't that high – you can't expect quality on the

cheap. And because of the quality it will last for a long time –
probably turning out eventually to have cost less than inferior
equipment. Then compact discs are so expensive; they're really
a waste of money unless you can get the best out of them. And
so we deaden the pain by mentally reducing Price and raising
the benefits of the Purpose. After a successful year or two in
America my friend will have no doubts about the wisdom of his
decision, and the benefit to his children.

Consistency

We have a great need to see ourselves as consistent. When
Kandinsky (as we saw in Chapter 1) argues that abstract
painting is no different from abstract music his argument
appeals because he is saying that you are not being consistent if
you accept the one and do not accept the other. Is it consistent
to agonise over allowing a brain-dead person to die by cutting
off the life-support machine, while being liberal on abortion?
Fortunately we are often able to keep inconsistent beliefs in
separate compartments so that we never have to see them side
by side – until, perhaps, the persuader asks us to do so.

Our response to inconsistency is either to accept it and
change our view, or to see clearly that the comparison is a false
one, or – most commonly – to use psychological accounting
to reduce the inconsistency. Thus, in the example above, the
father who sees going to the US as inconsistent with his duty
towards his children's education has to work quite hard at his
psychological accounting to reconcile the two.

Persuasion and price

If the skilled persuader realises, as he should, his own
propensity for restating Price through his programs he may
have a problem. It becomes harder to accept a rationalisation
when it is recognised for what it is. Psychological accounting
may not be as effective when you can see and understand the
process in action. Luckily the ability of people to fool
themselves is quite extensive and self-knowledge can be

overcome. But at least you have a choice. You can, so to speak, close your eyes while keeping them open.

> *One of my sons telephones me frequently about a decision he is thinking of making or an item he is thinking of buying. I used to probe him about his real reasons in the hope that he might take them into account. I have now given up. Not only does he take no notice, but I often find that he has already taken the decision or bought the item before phoning me. Nowadays I just give a vague paternal blessing in order to assist his psychological accounting, which is what he really wants.*

In the two-handed game the persuasion player's understanding of the assessment of Price will be invaluable, enabling him or her to stimulate the patterns needed for a satisfactory restatement and to suggest how the psychological accounting should be done.

First player   *So do you think you'll start the Open University course?*

Second player   *I'm not sure about it. It's a heck of a lot of work and it'll take at least four years.*

First player   *What do you do with your spare time now? After all, the study will be such a different experience from your job you may find the change relaxing.*

Second player   *That's true, I must say I usually waste my time off watching television or reading trashy novels.*

First player   *And you've often told me that most of the others at work have degrees. So it could prove a real advantage for the future.*

You will recognise that the first player is aiming to turn work into relaxation (using the frame of reference program); decreasing Price (the time Player 2 would lose through study was spare time anyway); and increasing the reward (future investment in job prospects). There is also an element of herd instinct coming into play: does the second player want to be the only person without a degree?

Remember that Pierpont Morgan spoke of the reason that 'sounds good'? Whatever the irrationality of the decision, however inappropriate the program which makes the Price acceptable, the second player must always end up with a reason that sounds good at the conscious level. We owe ourselves an adequate rationalisation and we are likely to need it to explain it to others.

LIGHTNING REMINDER

★ *Price comes in many forms; what will it cost your opponent?*

★ *Price can often be rationalised through psychological accounting – to satisfy consistency. You can help your opponent.*

PROBABILITY

The third point of the Motivation Triangle, Probability of success, still needs to be measured even if the balance between Purpose and Price is satisfactory. And the finer the balance the more confidence you will need in your eventual success.

People vary very much in their assessment of likely success, and we use the terms optimist and pessimist to categorise them – recognising that they have individual programs which form their general attitude to the outcome of events.

Characteristically, optimists have a belief in their capacity to control a situation, while pessimists believe that effects outside their control are likely to frustrate their plans. So we would

expect the optimist to give a high score to Probability of success
in the Motivation Triangle, while the pessimist – faced by the
same facts – will give a low score.

Who is right – the optimist or the pessimist?

> *In the UK successive governments have at different times
> subscribed to a range of economic theories. Each one has
> been proclaimed as the answer that will enable the
> country to sustain steady growth in prosperity without
> undue inflation or undue unemployment. And each one,
> after perhaps working for a time, has failed. At last some
> economists are beginning to acknowledge that we are
> very poor at predicting the outcome of such strategies
> and in fact know little about the effects of the actions at
> a government's disposal. Do you think that this reali-
> sation will alter the optimism of future chancellors of the
> exchequer?*

This is an example of what the psychologists call the 'illusion of
control' – which is a characteristic of optimists. A more trivial,
but easily tested, example, is that we value a lottery ticket much
more highly when it has a number we have chosen rather than
a random number. We know the chances are the same but our
brain programs cannot believe it.

> *The illusion of control operates in many areas. It is at its
> best in hindsight. That is, we are more inclined to take
> credit if an outcome is good – and blame outside factors
> if it isn't.*

Generally the facts of history support the pessimist. Imagine
someone living at the beginning of the twentieth century and
foreseeing the coming hundred years with a clear eye. How do
you think they would feel about the future? It is very difficult to

argue a person out of a depression – not because their views are irrational but because their view of events is likely to accord with the facts.

But the human race has to reject the pessimism program, however rational it may be. Think about a world in which everyone is a pessimist. Nothing would get done. Unless most people believe that on the whole things will turn out well, there would be no reason to attempt anything, no point in having ideals, no future for the human spirit. Depressives do not leap out in the morning to conquer the world; they retire to their beds and close the curtains.

The human organism itself needs optimism. At the physical level pessimists tend to be prone to poorer health, particularly as they grow older. And there is good evidence that people who feel in control of their lives enjoy better morale and live substantially longer.

> *A large-scale American study showed that new salespeople who were measured as having optimistic personalities had substantially greater chances of success than the pessimists. Sportspeople are similar.*

The optimism pattern remains powerful because it is essential. Optimism is a survival strategy for the human race.

Skilled persuaders may agree that circumstances and human nature have a habit of fouling up the best of human endeavours. But they know that there are still winners and losers. The skilled persuader as an individual can and will succeed. And they are probably right because they are successful players of what may be the most important persuasion game of all – auto-persuasion.

LIPS

LIPS stands for a phenomenon known as the limited image performance syndrome. The principle behind this syndrome is that our capacity for achievement is closely related to what we believe we can or ought to achieve. And it works both ways: it motivates us to reach the level of performance we have judged is right for us and it limits us from going any higher. The winning of the auto-persuasion game lies in raising the level of the image and therefore of the achievement.

> *Many life assurance salespeople are paid by commission. Their success tends to be related to the number of people they see, so therefore they can control their own earnings which can be as high as they choose.*
>
> *In practice they form an image of the amount of business they are capable of doing and stick quite closely to that. If they are provided with more competitive products or better sales equipment they may initially increase their performance, but it soon settles down. They may even lower their performance for a while to ensure that, over the whole period, they have not exceeded their LIPS.*
>
> *Their sales managers are much preoccupied in helping them to raise their LIPS because they know that it is the major determinant of success.*

Our self-image is formed by a combination of heredity and experience. While both of these continue to have an influence, image can be raised or lowered by a variety of means.

One way of defining image is the ranking order we recognise we are entitled to in the natural group to which we belong. Here both the herd instinct and the obedience program (see Chapter 3) play a part. For example a salesman whose score places him about midway in branch order will tend to maintain that position irrespective of the branch average. If he is moved from a mediocre branch to a very successful branch he will soon adjust his positioning so that he is midway in the order of the new branch. He will scarcely notice that his absolute score has increased.

Auto-persuaders who recognise this pattern in themselves will choose to mix with successful people. They make sure that the herd sets a high standard which they will find easier to follow than to fall behind. Similarly, in the two-handed game, the successful auto-persuader will parade examples of people who have achieved relevant success in order to give the other player confidence that they too can join the herd.

Success itself creates confidence, just as failure can do the opposite.

> *A month ago I met a friend who had just lost his important job. He was very upset, uncharacteristically incoherent and actually looked shrunken in size. A fortnight ago he told me that he had just been offered a new job at a higher salary and was off to the South Seas to spend his redundancy money. He actually looked bigger and he certainly felt it inside.*

The sales manager will try to establish as many ways of measuring success as possible – for instance an award for the top new person, an award for percentage of business remaining on the books, an award for single premium sales. The sales manager's aim is to find enough categories to enable the highest number of people to be good at something, knowing that even modest success can be built on.

Auto-persuaders parallel this by concentrating on looking at their achievements rather than at their failures. They may even keep a list of successes close at hand; when they feel their LIPS is falling they read their list to remind themselves of their potential. In the two-handed game they will, like the sales manager, seek out ways in which the other player can experience success.

> *The comedienne, Sally Duffell, remembers the time when, in despair following a disastrous performance,*

> *she went for help. 'I went to see a counsellor who made me run through all the best moments of my life. One of them was on stage, and I left thinking of 300 people screaming with laughter.'*
>
> *Her performance at the Hackney Empire the following night was a great success.*

Most people respond well to public recognition of their achievements. In fact they enjoy it so much that they raise their image to match up to the crowd's expectations of them. The sales manager will be ingenious in finding ways of making sure that success is publicised. The successful sales manager will use competitions, issue certificates of production standards, keep a prominent scoreboard of totals and issue a monthly magazine recording achievements.

The expectations of a respected individual are even more important for some people than recognition by the crowd. The sales manager will communicate to each salesperson the high opinion the sales manager has of their potential – that is, lending them a higher image of themselves until they have, so to speak, grown into it. The esteem of others is a powerful motivation; once we have it, we want to live up to it. Have you ever received a sincere congratulation from someone you respect without feeling the better and the bigger for it?

> *One successful sales manager told me how he had written over a hundred congratulatory messages to salespeople at the end of a good month. Every letter was personal, he told me, every letter was different. I know that was true because I still keep the letters he sent me; and the earliest ones go back over 35 years.*

'Every day, in every way, I am getting better and better.' That was the phrase which Doctor Coué advised his patients to repeat to themselves several times a day. Couéism was very popular in the 1920s – and deservedly so because auto-suggestion works. It may sound silly, but with constant repetition the idea infiltrates the subconscious and raises the image from within. It is the solo equivalent of the sales manager assuring the salesperson of their higher potential.

Today it is known as an 'affirmation'. The phrase you choose for yourself may be tailored to your own needs, but the principle is the same. Always affirm a positive statement – 'I will exceed my sales target with ease' – not a negative one, such as 'I will not fail to meet my sales targets'.

Beyond the techniques, the greatest value of understanding LIPS is the simple realisation that our achievements are not defined by our present capacities or our past history, but by the image that we have of ourselves. Raising the image cannot be done by snapping the fingers, but it can be done by a sensible application of the techniques which have been proved to work.

In the end the image we have is up to us to choose. Eleanor Roosevelt put it concisely: 'No one can make you feel inferior without your consent.'

LIGHTNING REMINDER

★ *Perception of probability of success is often more a function of temperament than facts.*

★ *High self-image increases optimism. Mix with the successful, keep your achievements prominent in your mind – and remember Coué.*

PERSISTENCE

With Purpose, Price and Probability balancing satisfactorily we are motivated to achieve: we take action. But at this point another program may appear that can erode that motivation.

It is reasonable to suppose that in the early development of our ancestors short-term decisions predominated over long-term ones. In hazardous situations those who fail to take care of the short term first don't have a long term. This programmed bias means that we give much greater importance to immediate rewards, even when they are small, than to long-term rewards, even when they are large. Faced by your twentieth visit to your maiden aunt in the hope of inheriting her fortune, the immediate tedium may begin to weigh more heavily than the benefits of becoming a millionaire in the remote future. The balance of the Motivational Triangle appears to change.

The best strategy to confound this program, or rather to employ it to help and not hinder, is to chop a lengthy task into segments, ensuring that each segment has its own reward. Then you have arranged a series of short terms which are steps towards the long term.

Some activities split naturally into segments. 'I am going to write a synopsis of my immortal novel; only when that's done will I think about producing the deathless prose' or 'I'll just get to know one or two of my neighbours first; then I expect they'll introduce me to other people'. Other activities may need a more artificial treatment: 'I'm only going to think about the next visit to my aunt; I'll take it one at a time.'

Rewards are important because they provide the short-term motivation. It's important to have them and to enjoy them as soon as possible after the achievement. Then they have the greatest psychological effect. You do not always have to construct artificial rewards because the completion of the task can often be sufficient reward in itself. If you make a neat job of decorating one room – perhaps the easiest one – it could give you the confidence to move to the next one. The reward and the confidence will be even stronger if one of your friends is impressed by your work.

Many years ago my wife and I decided to give up smoking for Lent. But we did it a week at a time – and smoking on Sundays was the reward for the

> *week's achievement. It worked, although we did tend to*
> *stay up chatting late on a Saturday, until midnight*
> *released us.*

Fulfilling a commitment is another form of reward. Weight Watchers, for example, depend on public commitment to a target — which will be generously acknowledged when it is achieved. A commitment to an individual, particularly when that individual is relying on its completion, is certainly powerful.

> *Cialdini describes an experiment in which a number of*
> *students were asked to attend a class at 7 a.m. Only*
> *about a quarter agreed. He then asked other students if*
> *they would attend the class, but he didn't mention the*
> *time. Over half agreed. When they were told about the*
> *time none of them withdrew their commitment and*
> *virtually all of them attended the class.*

Not being by nature a very persistent person I make great use of the commitment program as a self-motivator. I set and agree deadlines, which I am too proud to miss. I get meetings into my diary — sometimes months in advance — then I know I'll be there. I block in agreed times with my secretary, I even block in all my holiday dates at the beginning of the year, otherwise I'll miss them. It's not because I am an orderly person, it's because I am a disorderly person. I know I have to build the scaffolding of commitment, in order to motivate me to lay the bricks.

Action plans are described in some detail in my book *Managing People and Problems* but here are some basic points which can be readily adapted for any task where you want to bring about effective change:

- As a result of discussion, listening and thought you aim to arrive at the point where you understand the real nature of the change you want to make or the skill you want to acquire. Thus you have identified **Purpose**.

- Review the nature of the changes you will have to make in terms of behaviour. This is obviously necessary when you are acquiring a skill, but it also applies when you are dealing with feelings. You will not change feelings by attacking them directly; you must first understand and accept them, and then develop ways of behaving which gradually change them. Feeling follows behaviour. Changed behaviour is the **Price** you must pay.

- Devise a programme consisting of mini behaviour objectives which lead towards your **Purpose**. Tackle them one or two at a time, starting with the easiest. In this way you decrease the impact of **Price** and increase the **Probability** of success. See above for ideas on splitting tasks into sections to aid persistence.

- Check to see whether you will need outside help to succeed. For instance you might want more information, obtainable from a book or an organisation perhaps, or to attend, say, a course on assertiveness.

- Set yourself times to check on your progress. Rejoice in your successes and reward yourself. Readjust your programme where necessary and move on to the next mini goal with the confidence based on your earlier achievements.

- Action plans can be completed solo, but have a higher **Probability** if your partner or a friend is participating or supporting.

STRATEGIES FOR MOTIVATION

- Use the Motivation Triangle to analyse just what needs to be done if you want to motivate yourself or others. Remember that all three points must be adequately satisfied.

- Seek out the real **Purpose** for action and distinguish it from the ostensible purpose.

- Review **Price** and look at ways in which it might be presented at an acceptable level.

- Since the assessment of **Probability** is largely a function of
  temperament consider ways in which you can raise self-
  image.
    — Cultivate the company of successful people and so adopt
      their standards. Avoid the moaning minnies; they'll only
      infect you.
    — Keep your successes prominent in your mind and remind
      others of their successes. Learn lessons from your failures
      – then forget them.
    — Create a 'Coué' phrase and use it to train your
      subconscious.
- Tackle the need for **persistence** in completing a lengthy
  task, by using an action plan.
    — Split it into stages and concentrate on one at a time.
    — Find a reward for each stage – it may be an artificial
      reward or the reward of satisfaction.
    — Remember to provide the rewards, at least of generous
      acknowledgement, for those you are trying to motivate.
    — Look for opportunities to publicise your commitment
      among those whom you respect. You will not want to let
      them, or yourself, down.

3

Persuasion for the person who doesn't have to try

NATURAL AUTHORITY must seem to be a gift from the gods. But in fact you can acquire natural authority by mastering the ways in which authoritative people behave. And you can develop the attitudes of authority by raising your self-image in the ways we discussed in the previous chapter. Add to this the methods which make your communications immediately believable and you are well on the way to winning the persuasion game.

LIKE MANY GAMES, persuasion has its trump cards. While sheer ingenuity of play will often win the trick, it can be useful and sometimes essential to pre-empt the normal routines and play trumps.

There are two closely connected kinds of trumps in the game — one is personal authority and the other is credibility. If you are a good player you will ensure that you have both of these, and know exactly how and when to play them for maximum effect. You will develop their power because your opponent may also be carrying trumps; you must make sure that you rank higher.

In this chapter I want to look first at personal authority, or dominance, and then discuss credibility.

PERSONAL AUTHORITY

There are many kinds of power: the power to force compliance through, say, a machine gun or a truncheon; the power which comes from rank; the power which comes from controlling desirable resources, like deciding salaries or having the key to the sweetie cupboard; and the power that comes from superior knowledge. We can see immediately why these are effective. But the power of personal authority is different. And that is our primary concern in winning the persuasion game. Some people appear to get their own way with no more backing than their own personalities. How does this come about; can it be cultivated?

The power of personal authority depends on the deep instinct human beings have for obedience. This has been confirmed by many psychologists, but the classic experiment was carried out by Professor Stanley Milgram at Yale University.

The Milgram experiment

Professor Milgram wanted to find out just how willing people would be to inflict physical pain when they were requested to do so by someone ostensibly in authority. The experiment involved asking volunteers to give higher and higher electric shocks to other volunteers every time they made a mistake in answering a series of questions. The experts he consulted beforehand predicted that about 98 per cent of the volunteers would refuse to go above trivial levels. I wonder how high *we* would have been prepared to go − 50 volts? 75 volts? Up to 100 volts? − if someone asked us firmly enough?

The results of the experiment were surprising. Despite the

howls and screams of the victims, two out of three volunteers were prepared to go the whole way, that is, up to 450 volts – well above the point on the dial marked 'Danger: severe shock'.

Of course *we* would have been the one out of three who would have refused. But the fact was that *all* the volunteers were prepared to go as high as 300 volts – substantially higher than domestic voltage. What's more, Milgram got the same results from all his volunteers, irrespective of the gender, religion or ethnic background.

(Just in case you were worried, I should point out that the victims were, of course, all collaborators of Milgram. Unbeknown to the volunteer, no electric shocks were actually being inflicted.)

The circumstances of the Milgram experiment were unusual. But suppose you are a hospital nurse who is telephoned by a doctor you have not met, and asked to give medication to a patient. The rules of the hospital say you must not do this without a written instruction. When you go to the cabinet you find the doctor has told you to give a dose twice as high as the maximum clearly stated on the label.

Would you administer the medication?

No, of course not! But 19 out of 20 nurses did. Luckily it was an experiment in obedience and the medication was in fact a placebo.

Such experiments show us why personal authority is such a powerful trump card. If you can develop your authority, you are able to ride to victory on the human brain program of obedience, which most people do not remotely suspect they have.

SELF-DEFENCE AGAINST THE OBEDIENCE PROGRAM

- First, accept that you are probably subject to the obedience program and therefore over-susceptible to the authority of others.
- Cultivate *anti-obedience* habits; unless your attitude is habitual you will be caught out one day – or even every day. Here are the key habits.
  - Always ask yourself whether the 'authority' has a genuine right to tell you what to do. If they haven't *you* decide.
  - Never assume a regulation exists unless it clearly does, and does so by lawful authority.
  - Look for opportunities to be intelligently disobedient; it will become easier with practice. (Remember how Nelson, when ordered to withdraw his ships at the Battle of Copenhagen, put his telescope to his blind eye and was unable to see the signal.)
  - If your instinct tells you that something is wrong, or stupid, or unnecessary, it probably is. Pause and examine your instincts before acting. There is only one authority which we must all obey – our own, carefully formed, judgements.
- High personal authority is inconsistent with the obedience program. Therefore the development of high personal authority, as described below, is an important strategy.

Is personal authority inherited?

One might expect this to be so because every group would need to have, say, one person in ten with a capacity to dominate. The necessary genes would have been transmitted because the leader of the primitive group would have acquired a larger number of mates with whom to breed.

An interesting experiment was carried out with deer mice. They were kept in small groups and the dominant animal was identified. At the second stage the offspring of the mice were put into groups; the progeny of a dominant parent were significantly more likely to be dominant in their own groups.

Another factor in dominance appears to be hormonal. People with high levels of testosterone tend to be more active and more dominating. The thrust of testosterone may push someone towards a life of crime or towards success in their profession, depending on their backgrounds or their choices.

While inheritance would play a part in this, it is not the whole story. Cadets at the military academy of West Point in America were found to have levels of testosterone corresponding to their seniority. In the first year, when they were treated as inferior forms of life by their seniors, levels were low. The highest levels were found among the cadets of the senior year, whose members ruled the roost.

In some experiments the hormone levels were tested in team players after a contest or game. There were marked differences between the team which had just won and the team which had just lost.

So it seems likely that starting with the right level of hormone will help you towards high personal authority, but success and dominance will themselves increase the level of hormones needed.

Being a loser in life can be very stressful because you are always trying to cope with events which you can't control. For instance, middle management in business is more stressful than top management because you suffer the pressures without adequate power to deal with them.

The effects of continued stress on the hormone system can be to keep the heart rate high, even during sleep, and to reduce general resistance to disease.

In whatever way the genes of dominance are distributed in a population, I am sure that many people possess the gene but do not use it. The obedience program thus takes precedence. The dominance program is likely to be latent within us until circumstances call it forth. Or, in the case of persuasion players, until they call it forth for themselves.

LIGHTNING REMINDER

★ *Personal authority is a powerful card in the persuasion game because of the obedience program.*

★ *Learn to defend yourself against your opponents' authority by cultivating defensive strategies.*

LIPS and dominance

Abraham Maslow, a distinguished psychologist, studied many of the dimensions of personal authority. He then looked for some comparatively simple method of measurement which could be used as a rough and ready guide to status. He found it in self-image. Those who, by the scientific measurements, had been graded as having dominant status had high respect for themselves, a feeling of superiority, and a confidence that they could deal with most people and most situations they would meet. People with low dominance saw themselves at the other end of the scale on all these counts. So an essential first step towards dominance is to ensure that you raise your LIPS; methods for doing this were described in the last chapter.

Who has the problem?

Another attitude associated with dominance is a refusal to take responsibility for other people's problems. This is best explained by an example.

Suppose that the woman who does your cleaning has become

unpunctual and careless. Your problem is to ensure that the house, or the office, is properly cleaned. So, after giving her due warning and an opportunity to improve, you sack her. Then you find a good replacement and dismiss the incident from your mind. At least you do if you are a dominant person. If not, you delay sacking her as long as possible and, if you can bring yourself eventually to do so, there is an unpleasant and apologetic interview. After she has gone you feel guilty and wonder whether you should have helped her find another job. In other words, you have taken on her problem as well as your own.

The habit of taking on other people's problems is present in many people. Do I pick up my husband's clothes when he has trailed them across the floor? Do I tell my wife the truth when she really, really asks me to say honestly whether I like her new dress? Do I get rid of that old man who rambles on during my charity committees? The opportunities for taking on other people's problems are legion. Here are some examples you may recognise; no doubt you can think of many more.

- You get bad service in a shop or restaurant, but you like the server and you don't complain.
- The only seat in the train is filled by the huge haversack of the traveller sitting beside it. You prefer to stand rather than to ask for it to be removed.
- It's your partner's turn to do the washing up and take the dog for a walk. But if your partner delays long enough you find yourself doing it.
- When you were interviewed for the job you were promised an office to yourself. Your employers turn out to be charming but you find yourself sharing an office. What do you do?
- You have made a bet with a friend and you win. But your friend never volunteers to pay up and you don't like to chase him. Who has the problem?

We all find it very easy to think up reasons for not taking action. But it's important to distinguish between a good reason and moral cowardice. If you don't act it may be because you would be embarrassed by a scene, or because you want to be thought of as a nice guy, or because you're afraid the other person may get their revenge. But once we've faced up to our true motives it becomes possible first to kick ourselves and then kick the problem back to the person to whom it belongs.

It is not that dominant people are heartless, it's that they believe that the world works best if they solve the problems which are their own responsibility and do not distract themselves with the problems which are the responsibility of other people.

You will not be surprised by the fact that many apparently tenderhearted people turn out to be quite tough when they act at one remove. Business consultants are paid high fees for being stalking horses who recommend redundancies. How could the kindest management go against their recommendations? The percentage of people in the Milgram experiment who would apply the maximum voltage increased to 93 per cent when they did not throw the 'punishment' switch themselves, but merely threw the switch which signalled an intermediary to do so.

This is why dominant people do not feel guilty when the tenderhearted chide them for their ruthlessness.

Defining the social situation

High dominance people tend to define the social situation. They will often speak first, establishing both the topic of conversation and its level. They may not speak frequently, allowing their inferiors to chatter on, but they continue to guide the social transactions with gentle touches to which the rest respond.

By convention we allow the host or hostess the position of dominance on their own territory so that they can carry out this function. The interviewer is allowed to guide the conversation, although dominant interviewees will sometimes bite back to remind them that they are only enjoying a privilege by favour.

Signs and signals

Height and carriage

In the lower animals there is often a correlation between size and dominance, although this is not invariable. When physical strength is a key factor in defending a position, you would expect the naturally larger animal to be higher up the scale.

As the story of estimating the height of the university professor in Chapter 1 demonstrates, this association still remains in human beings. Many studies have shown that tall people have a greater than average chance of getting into superior positions. Human beings will also increase their size artificially. Heavy robes, policemen's helmets, bishops' mitres, conducting a meeting from a platform are all devices we use to achieve dominance.

Carriage also conveys dominance. The upright stance with head held high gives a different message from the bowed head and the curved back. Indeed it is hard to maintain upright carriage and feel inferior. Try it and see.

Gaze

It has often been observed among social animals that the inferior ranks spend much more time watching the leader than the leader does watching them. It's a good strategy because as a follower you need to know what you should be doing next. Similarly, lower ranking human beings will gaze at the leader to pick up the clues for action or response they need in order to fulfil their obedience program.

I used to attend a meeting at which the boss, himself a dominant man, circulated the chairmanship of the

> *discussion among his executives. Any observant visitor could detect the real leader even though the chairman had ostensible authority. The visitor only had to notice how everyone's eyes flickered towards the boss rather than the chairman in order to get guidance for their reactions.*

Leaders use gaze too, but in a different way. It is more of a fixed gaze and it is reserved for occasions when they want to make a point or confirm their authority. Otherwise, their gaze is likely to be broader and roaming; like any leader they need to be aware of what is going on so that they can control and secure the group.

> *A dominant person will use a firm gaze on meeting someone for the first time. In less than a second she will have conveyed her higher status and the other person will have accepted this without any realisation of what has happened.*

Relaxation

One might expect a leader to be a little on edge with all that responsibility; they will be tensed for action. But this is in fact the sign of the inferior person who is always looking to gain position, always concerned that they may lose it. Dominance and confidence go together, so the leader is relaxed. That does not stop them from being watchful, nor from springing into firm action on the instant. Watch a dominant cat as it strolls with supreme relaxation around its territory, then notice the change when an intruder appears.

> *It has been observed that the dominant rooster in a flock is easy to handle, apparently feeling confident about any situation he might face. The lowest ranking bird will be irritable and difficult to handle; tension and strain are suggested by all his actions.*

Clothes

The spectacular markings of some fish, the impressive feathers of some birds and the development of huge, if unwieldy, antlers by the stag are the equivalents of human dominance clothes. And just as the appearance varies with the species, so human dominance clothes vary with the setting and the expectations of the audience.

> *In an experiment in Texas the psychologist's collaborator would walk across the street against the lights. The psychologist then counted how many people took his lead. When he was wearing a business suit on average 3.5 times as many people followed him compared with when he was wearing T-shirt and jeans.*

A business suit may carry authority in those circumstances. In offices it is often easy to detect by their clothes which women have executive status or ambitions and which do not. In the Milgram experiment the 'authority figure' wore a grey, technician's coat. A policeman's uniform or a parson's collar are other familiar examples of particular authority. Of course con artists know this too.

Developing the traits of dominance

Dominance is conveyed and recognised through behaviour, but ultimately it depends on attitude of mind. You have to *want* to have personal authority and to be convinced of your own ability to be the natural one in charge if you want to sustain a dominant attitude over any length of time. But, just as our internal feelings can change our behaviour, so our behaviour can change our feelings. I gave an example earlier when I said that it was difficult to maintain an upright carriage and feel inferior at the same time. Try it again now.

Height and carriage

> *Try standing up straight in a military posture and say to yourself out loud: 'I am a louse, I am lower than nothing, I am a wimp.' You'll find that the words simply don't fit. Then try standing in a humble position, shoulders slumped, twisting your hands, and say: 'I can do anything, I like a challenge, I'm in charge.'*

If you develop the carriage of personal authority and make it a habit, it will feed through your subconscious and change not only the way that people respond to you but how you think about yourself. Why do parents tell their children to sit up straight? Because they recognise, at least instinctively, that they are guiding them towards behaviour which will give them status.

Relaxation

Relaxation is similar. It takes longer to learn than good carriage but you will find instructions to help you in the books mentioned in the *Useful Reading* list at the end of this book. Learning to relax is not just a physical change, the effects on one's whole mental outlook can be profound. In developing the confidence and sense of control that comes with relaxation you are developing important attributes of personal authority.

Gaze

You may like to experiment with gaze. Go carefully because gaze can easily convey either a desire for intimacy or an aggressive threat. It's a point to which we will return in Chapter 4.

Dress

Dress provides a good example of the effect of actions on feelings. Both men and women tend to find that being dressed to their satisfaction gives a sense of confidence. Even the process, lengthy in some cases, of choosing dress and accessories may be a ritual needed to prepare the mind for coping with challenges. For books in this area, see the *Useful Reading* list on page 259.

Can you stand the heat?

There is one further hurdle to leap and it is the highest of all. Since in every grouping authority figures are in the minority, it is a lonely position. There is a gap, not just of distance but also of quality, between those who lead and those who follow. It does not make for easy intimacy.

True authority figures, as opposed to bullies, are well mannered, considerate and often charming. Like the top rooster they have no need to be anything else. But they are *different*; if you can't live with that then you can't be an authority figure. It comes with the territory.

STRATEGIES FOR DEVELOPING PERSONAL AUTHORITY

- Work at developing a high self-image using the methods described in the last chapter.

- Don't be imposed upon; don't impose upon yourself. Only take on *your* problems. Refuse all substitutes.
- In social circumstances be the person who defines the situation; after all, you *are* the leader.
- Develop the signs of dominance: height and carriage, gaze, relaxation, clothes. The others will respond through their obedience program.
- Steel yourself to accept that personal authority separates you from those without it. Tough but true.

CREDIBILITY

Personal authority is the kind of trump card which you carry with you wherever you go, although you do not have to use it when submissiveness is the best strategy. Credibility is a card which you play as you need it. Its techniques can be clearly seen by thinking of it as a card played against you. In looking at it from this point of view it is easier to judge its possible effects and to understand either how to develop them or how to counter them. Credibility programs apply very directly in public speaking; we will look at the topic again in Chapter 5.

The relevant credentials

You would be readier to believe a nuclear physicist speaking about atomic fallout than a taxi driver; just as a taxi driver would be more credible on local traffic conditions. Your opponents make sure that you know their qualifications so that you will give due weight to what they say.

People are hungry for qualifications. I received a letter from a friend of mine and noticed that he had sprouted the letters FIPS (Fellow of the Institute of Profession Salesmen). I asked him how he had earned this

> *impressive credential. 'I filled an application form and sent a cheque,' he replied. Some magazines carry advertisements for a number of American educational institutions who appear to be ready to provide senior qualifications on much the same basis.*

And my friend may be relying on your use of the program which inclines us to take such credentials for granted. For instance the word 'doctor' carries an aura of authority in medical or quasi medical matters and even beyond. But medical doctors come in different grades and sizes. According to their particular expertise their opinion may be valuable or it may be no more reliable than a layperson's. And even specialists can disagree. Trevor Sheldon of the University of York, an authority on such matters, tells us that about 80 per cent of all medical interventions have never been properly evaluated.

Beware the outside expert; distance lends enchantment. The best definition of an expert I have heard is 'the person from the next village'. Think about the program which leads us to give credence to an imported outsider in preference to someone we already know. As the scriptures say: 'A prophet is not without honour, except in his own country.' In Chapter 9 you will read more about the value of experts.

If you want to put your ideas across but do not have the right credentials, or cannot present the credentials you have in a form which carries weight, your next move is to support your case by quoting from the relevant authorities. This can be just as convincing. However this ploy must be carefully watched. How authoritative are the authorities? Did they actually say what you claim – and without qualifications? Are there other authorities who disagree? What weight did you give to the authority of Trevor Sheldon, or the scriptures, in the paragraphs you have just read?

Straightening out the bias

Suppose you hear a trade unionist arguing forcefully why workers should get more share of the cake. You might be inclined to dismiss some of the force of the argument because of the trade unionist's natural bias. But suppose you heard a trade unionist arguing that more profits should be retained in the business, you will prick up your ears. Because the trade unionist is arguing apparently against his own interests you are inclined to believe him. But his arguments are good or bad according to his reasoning and his evidence, not according to his bias or lack of it.

The skilled persuader will often take up an unexpected position on a subject in order to ride on this effect. Watch very carefully. It may be a manoeuvre allowing him or her to creep around the back of your mind while you are accepting their patent honesty at the front.

> *If you were writing an advertisement comparing your product with its competitors you might be tempted to demonstrate its superiority on every relevant point. But that would be unwise. A more persuasive advertisement would show superiority on some points and admit equality on others. The credibility gained through your honesty makes the whole advertisement more believable.*

Your opponent, having demonstrated his or her honesty, reinforces it by facing up squarely to the arguments against their position. And your opponent is wise to do so. Unless your opponent thinks that you're inclined to be on their side anyhow, he knows that he must acknowledge the opposing arguments and refute them if he is to convince you. Watch how your opponent does it. While he gives plenty of time for his own arguments to sink in, he moves on quickly once he has explained the opposing view so that you don't really have time to think about it. And he will probably deal with this view in the middle of what he is saying because he knows that people retain best what they hear at the beginning and the end – he will reserve those privileged positions for his own strongest points.

Are you sitting comfortably?

Imagine that your opponent is trying to sell you an insurance policy for accidental death. She might put forward one of two types of argument. The first would be factual, for example: 'The Office of Population Censuses and Surveys' figures tell us that half the deaths that occur to adults under 35 are accidental.' Alternatively, she might simply tell you a story about a policyholder of hers who died by accident, and how proud she felt when she was able to present the widow with a large cheque.

Which is the more credible argument?

It must be the first, mustn't it? This is an objective statistic which gives us an accurate picture of the probability of accidental death; the second is merely an anecdote which gives us no useful information at all. The rational mind has to go for the facts.

But that doesn't allow for the brain program through which we identify with a story. It captures our imagination; it captures our feelings. It is an example of the prominence program, described in Chapter 1, where a dramatic fact in the forefront of the mind has a stronger influence than the full, rational picture. And it has been demonstrated by experiments that the story is likely to be more persuasive than the statistic. So be on your guard against stories – although you might like to use some yourself when it's you who are playing the credibility trump.

Josef Stalin once observed: 'One death is a tragedy, a million is a statistic.' He was simply reflecting on the power that a single concrete instance has over the imagination. In the summer of 1993 the injuries of one five-year-old girl in Sarajevo triggered an international rescue operation. Yet, prior to Operation Irma, the statistics of deaths and injuries to children in former Yugoslavia were well known. But they were not prominent.

Like likes like

> *I often speak to audiences of salespeople about the psychology of persuasion. Usually it's not to members of my own company because it's easier for me to be the 'person from the next village'. I am able to present my credentials because I am fortunate enough to have risen, with the passage of time, to a senior marketing position and because I have written books on the subject. But I always make sure my audience know that I spent many years myself as a salesman and I can see the world from their point of view.*

That is a very credible combination; it combines a level of relevant authority with a similarity to my audience. They know that I am sympathetic towards them and, by reciprocation, they are sympathetic towards me. We like people who are similar to us and we trust the people whom we like. Provided that similarity is relevant to the topic it increases credibility.

Beware

Beware of the opponents you like. The equation that makes liking equal trust and trust equal credibility is a deep brain program. So, when you like someone be suspicious of yourself; make allowances for the probability that you are giving them more credence than objectively they merit.

We like people who share a common background with us – perhaps we went to the same school or came from the same town. We like people if we have common friends and common interests. We like people who have the same attitudes as we do. If your opponent is skilled he or she will tune in to these factors and use them to draw out your liking.

Mostly we like people who are humorous and make us laugh. Your skilled opponent, if he has any talent for this, will use it on you. And he will gauge the level and type of humour you appreciate. If he comes across just as a 'funny man' you may write him off as a clown. If he uses bawdy humour which you find unacceptable your liking will go into reverse. But if it's well judged you will find it hard to resist liking him – and the rest of the equation follows.

It's not surprising that we tend to like attractive people. What is surprising is how deep that program goes. It starts very early: not only do adults tend to favour and excuse attractive children, but children themselves favour their more attractive playmates.

It continues through life. In Chapter 1 I described how attractive people were twice as likely to be found not guilty as unattractive people. I could have added that in civil lawsuits attractive people get awarded larger damages than the unattractive. Attractive students tend to get better grades than unattractive students. There are many other examples. For instance, if you want to get a petition signed use attractive canvassers; they are more successful. And if you want to be a politician reflect on this:

> *In the 1974 Canadian federal elections attractive candidates received 2½ times as many votes as unattractive candidates. Yet the voters were quite unaware of the program that was directing them; in follow-up interviews three-quarters of them specifically denied that this was a factor they had taken into account.*

As if that wasn't enough, we even speak differently to attractive people, and they, not surprisingly, reciprocate by speaking charmingly to us in return. Life, unless you happen to be attractive, is very unfair. There must be a defence somewhere.

Defence against the credibility trump

Luckily there is. The first line of defence is that credibility programs tend to be skin deep. That is, they have their strongest effect when the argument is not one in which we are really involved or about which we know a good deal. In fact some of the programs actually go into reverse when this is the case.

For example, if we agree with someone's point of view it may help if his or her way of presenting the arguments is incompetent. We find ourselves mentally supplying the points he or she has missed or thinking how much better we could present the case. In that process we become even more deeply attached to our own opinion. Similarly, most of the studies which show the advantage of attractiveness have been concerned with issues that do not really engage our interest or attention. Trials and elections are, of course, important but that does not mean that we are prepared to devote hard rational thought to our decisions. And, of course, the initial effects of attractiveness wear off quite quickly if the goods we expect are not delivered according to description. Indeed, our disillusion may be all the stronger because we feel we've been had.

The second line of defence is to be aware of the programs which create credibility. Look out for them, make allowances for them. You may even want to familiarise yourself with them by experimenting with the techniques – always in a good cause, of course. Like winning a game or two.

CREDIBILITY STRATEGIES

- Clarify your qualifications. If you haven't got any, then quote from those who have.
- To avoid apparent bias be ready to argue against your own position. But then turn this to your advantage.
- Remember that the motivational stories carry more credibility than dry, objective facts. Use them often.
- Present yourself as similar to your opponent; the more they can identify with you the more they will be ready to believe.
- Look for ways to help your opponent to like you. Humour helps, so does attractiveness.
- Your best defence against credulity is to be on your guard against the points above. Remember that you always have the capacity to use the manual override on your mental camera (see Chapter 1).

4

Persuasion without words

NON VERBAL COMMUNICATION is the music behind the words. You can learn how to read your opponents' feelings and reactions so that you can respond effectively; you can learn how to transmit persuasive messages without your opponent even being aware of what is happening. You can avoid the negative non verbal communication which can destroy your case — without you ever knowing why.

WHAT IS YOUR NATIVE LANGUAGE? Before you answer English or French or Swahili, remember that this is a trick question. The only language we were actually born with is the language of non verbal communication.

As babies we were able to communicate pain and pleasure, and soon developed our vocabulary to include fear, loneliness, amusement, discomfort and a wide range of other feelings. Later we learnt to show that we wanted this toy rather than that, or the strength of our feelings about a particular brand of food. In fact, by the time we uttered our first recognisable word, we had become skilled communicators through non verbal means. We were not only using it to convey messages, we also understood it well enough to interpret the messages of others.

Non verbal communication (NVC) covers a large field such as facial expression, body posture, gestures, touch, clothes, tone of voice and use of territory. It can be an explicit substitute for speech, as when we nod our heads in agreement or point at a wanted object, or it can be an implicit running accompaniment to our communication of which we may be fully or partially unaware.

TEST YOURSELF ON NVC

1.   You watch two people talking in a café. They seem to touch each other a great deal during the conversation. Are they likely to be:

     English? South American? French?

2.   You are in negotiation – which you thought was going quite well. Then the other party unbuttons his jacket. Is he:

     Feeling too hot? About to bop you one? Keen on your ideas?

3.   You see two photographs of twins. Although they are identical you find one more attractive than another. Is this:

     Sheer chance? You like the photo you saw first? Something to do with the eyes?

4.   Driving on the main road you become aware that the car behind is right on your tail; it makes you feel angry. Is this because:

     It's dangerous? Your space is being invaded? Combination of both?

5. In conversation with a new friend you notice that they look at you a lot. Are they:

    Showing they like you? Trying to make you like them? Just curious?

Intriguing isn't it? As you study this chapter you will find out whether you were right. Or, perhaps, both right and wrong at the same time . . .

NVC AND PERSUASION

Skilled persuasion players are primarily concerned with implicit NVC. They think of it as the music behind the words. They know that most people hear this music only faintly, but these players have taken the trouble to train their ears so that they understand the score.

This is a big advantage because it not only gives them a superior understanding of how their opponents are feeling but it enables them to transmit, through their own NVC, the messages they choose. We saw this in the context of dominance in the last chapter.

Imagine yourself in the middle of a persuasion game. As your opponent is speaking you can read surtitles over his head which say things like: 'I'm really interested in that idea, just another push and I'll agree', or 'I know I'm speaking pleasantly to you but actually I don't like you and your ideas, and I'd prefer to leave the room', or 'I was indifferent to you at first, but as our conversation has gone on I've come to like you more and more'. It's like being able to see the cards in your opponent's hand, while concealing your own.

When couples first come to marriage counselling they usually sit quite close together. They are more scared of the counsellor than they dislike each other. As the

> *interviews progress and the couple's difficulties emerge*
> *they lean further and further away from each other. As*
> *the healing process starts they gradually begin to move*
> *back towards each other. When they are once more*
> *sitting close and parallel the counsellor knows they are*
> *ready to go it alone, without further help.*

THE ORIGINS OF NVC

The basis of NVC is innate – a set of inherited programs. We know this because there are many close parallels between the NVC of animals – particularly primates – and humans; and because many aspects of NVC are common between widely separated races and cultures.

However, this foundation vocabulary is soon modified by cultural programs; for example, the Japanese control facial expressions of tension in public, while showing them in private, and the gestures of Italians are different from those of northern Europeans.

> *Couples were systematically observed in cafés and the*
> *number of times they touched per hour was counted.*
> *Puerto Ricans touched 180 times; Parisians touched 110*
> *times. The English score was zero.*

Cultural differences are very important for travellers or those doing business with foreigners. For instance, Arabs in conversation stand much closer to one another than the English – who are made uncomfortable by too much proximity. English people can be seen retreating over several yards before this invasion of their privacy if they have not been previously warned that no invasion is intended.

People develop personal programs too. By definition these

cannot be generalised but over a period of acquaintance individual NVC can be noted, giving an additional strand of communication. Learning the 'dialect' that an individual has developed will give you a good basis for interpreting their NVC with increased accuracy.

> *Professional NVC trainers will sometimes use video to help their students study their own NVC. It can be very revealing. Home videoing can be helpful here, provided you remember that our behaviour can change when we are 'on show'.*

THE POWER OF NVC

The power of NVC does not derive only from the fact that unskilled people use the language without realising they are doing so, or interpret the language of others unconsciously, but in its prevailing effect. That is, NVC is a more reliable indicator of feeling than verbal communication and people respond to this. When, for example, people express a feeling in words, but their NVC expresses an opposite feeling, it is the NVC which people believe – and they are right to do so.

LEARNING NVC

NVC is not a parlour trick. A single sign is rarely a reliable measure of feeling taken on its own. The observer must watch for a cluster of signs, noting any which seem to contradict the general picture; and relate these signs to the verbal language when it is being used. Ideally, as I suggest above, an observer should watch an individual over a period of time to make sure they have mastered the individual's particular dialect.

> *A group of managers was being trained in group NVC and the instructor pointed out that one man was showing by the way he turned his body away from the group that he did not feel part of it. He replied that he had injured his pelvis in a sports accident many years before and was therefore obliged to sit at that angle. Had the instructor watched his other signals, he would have avoided a silly mistake.*

He will also need to study some full texts on NVC, and I make some suggestions in the *Useful Reading* list. In this chapter I will only be giving a flavour of the possibilities. But book study alone is just the start. If you are to be a good persuasion player, you must become a continuous and acute observer of NVC under a variety of conditions, and you must observe, practise and experiment with your own NVC.

Learning a language takes time, although a real improvement in NVC can be achieved quite quickly. But it's worth it. Most foreign languages are only used on an occasional basis, but NVC will be used the whole time. Like other languages it can lapse with disuse; the skilled persuader is constantly working to improve the fluency of both their reception and their transmission.

LIGHTNING REMINDER

★ *NVC is a language we knew as babies; adults forget its importance.*

★ *With good NVC you can receive and transmit information hidden from your opponent.*

★ *NVC is inherited, but it is modified by different cultures or by different personal programs.*

★ *NVC is more truthful about feelings than words.*

★ *Although NVC is easier than a foreign language you will only master it through study and observation. The rewards are high.*

LIKING AND DISLIKING

Liking, as the last chapter described, equates with trust; therefore stimulating liking is an important technique for the persuader. Beyond trust, of course, lies our wish to accommodate people we like and to be of service to them. To study this, imagine you are observing, but not hearing, a couple who are getting on together.

We would expect them to smile a good deal and reciprocate each other's expression and nods. But since facial expressions can be too easily faked the evidence will be unreliable. But we do notice that they look at each other quite a lot because mutual gaze is a characteristic of friendly relations. The listener at any moment is more likely to be gazing than the speaker.

If they were able to choose their seating positions they are probably at an oblique angle to one another; though, if they were just sharing each other's company without much conversation, they might be side by side. If they are standing, and can therefore choose their distance, they will probably be quite close – perhaps 2 to 4 feet.

Their general posture will be open to one another and, if they are men, jackets will be unbuttoned. Interestingly, their postures will tend to mirror each other so that, for instance, if one has an elbow on the table the other will do too. Then, if one changes his position, shortly afterwards the other will move in imitation. Mirroring your customer is a well-known silent sales technique.

You can easily experiment with mirroring posture. When you are in friendly conversation change your posture by, for instance, putting your elbow on the table. See how long it takes for your friend to follow suit. Then change back to your original posture and see what happens. If mirroring does not take place your friend may not be quite as friendly as you suppose!

Cultivating liking

How would you, the skilled persuader, use this information to cultivate liking in someone you had recently met? First, you would be cautious; if you move too far ahead of your opponent you will lose the game, and the pay-off will be dislike or defensiveness. So you will work gradually, being highly sensitive to whether you get a reciprocal response. Your initial proximity will be perhaps 4 to 5 feet, and you will only move in a foot or so as the conversation warms. You will deliberately use eye contact (which is not the same as staring), particularly when listening, because this not only expresses liking, it also tends to induce it in return. You will be aware that women naturally use more eye contact than men, and so you will interpret this with proper tact.

If the original sitting position is face to face – a challenging orientation unless in a formal situation like a restaurant – you should try for an oblique position; you may even have an item to show your companion to provide an excuse for changing to a more favourable orientation. You will look out for mirroring of posture and may even try a new posture to see if your opponent will follow. If you are able to work through to this stage you have won the non verbal friendship game and the pay-off is a fruitful relationship.

As a conversation progresses speakers synchronise their dialogue so that they know when the one has finished speaking and the other can start. For instance, a speaker who wishes to carry on may signal this by a hand gesture or by momentarily avoiding the other's eye. When the speaker is ready to stop his hand drops, he catches the other's eye and his conversation slows and his voice drops as he concludes. This may be in response to an interposing hand or body movement from the person wishing to speak, who will accompany this by holding the other's eye. It's a skilled but unconscious process – almost a kind of dance.

> *One senior executive used to give the signals of someone who had finished speaking when he was still in mid-thought. As a result he was constantly interrupted and would become quite tetchy after a while – before his subordinates learnt his idiosyncrasy.*

YOU INTEREST ME

The persuader will often want to know whether a suggestion or a proposition he or she has made interests the other person. One obvious sign may be that the listener leans forward, closing the gap, and livens up. This may be the point when the listener unbuttons his jacket (if he is a man) in order to get down to things. The listener's eyes will open wider and, if really hooked, the pupils will dilate.

> *Dilation of the pupils is an interesting phenomenon most often associated with interest in the opposite sex. Men, shown two, apparently identical, photographs of an attractive woman, will habitually choose the one in which the pupils of the eye have been artificially dilated. But they will rarely be aware of the reasons for their choice. At one time women used to dose their eyes with belladonna (literally 'beautiful woman'), or deadly nightshade, to make themselves more appealing.*

DEFENSIVENESS AND DISAGREEMENT

The signs of defensiveness and disagreement can be inferred from the absence of the signals for liking and interest I have described. But some additional points may be noted.

> *I called one of my staff in for a personnel interview. I knew him to be a rather defensive person. He arrived bearing a large sheet of artwork which he kept on his knees in front of him rather like a chest protector. So I continued a friendly conversation until he felt at ease enough to put his protection down; then it was time to start the interview.*

Not everyone carries such an obvious protection, so the skilled persuader must look out for other signals, which might be broadly described as closed gestures. Examples would be folded arms, especially if the hands are clenched and tense, and crossed legs. The body may be leaning away from you. The jacket (of a man) is likely to remain buttoned.

Inconsistencies can be very revealing. Behind the open, unbuttoned jacket may lie a closely buttoned waistcoat protected by a watch chain. What would you make of that? Your companion may be facing you, in friendly fashion, with the top half of his body — while the bottom half is turned away. Sometimes it will be turned in the direction of the door suggesting, perhaps, that your companion would like to leave you if it were possible. This might be reinforced with a tapping foot. There are other common gestures which seem to say exactly what they mean. For instance hand over mouth can be an expression of surprise (symbolically checking the gasp), or a sign of nervousness about what one is saying, or to emphasise its confidentiality.

Facial expression poses problems because it can be easily faked, although a negative expression can usually be taken at 'face value'. But consider a friend of mine who sometimes appears to be listening intently to me – until I notice that he is leaning back and his face is tense and immobile. I know he's going to disagree long before I've finished. When he likes what I'm saying his face is mobile and relaxed.

As a skilled persuader you must be alive to these negative signals and respond by changing tack. You know that you have more and different work to do in order to unlock the defences. Then you can move forward again.

The portable lie-detector

The conventional lie-detector measures changes in the body such as heart rate, blood pressure and electrical changes in the skin – because these respond automatically to the emotions involved in telling a lie. The parallel is quite close because the operator must first establish the subject's natural responses and only then can the abnormal response be identified – just as the NVC observer increases accuracy through familiarity with the subject's normal behaviour. Lie-detector readings can be faked by a skilled subject with good control over their emotions; and so can NVC. Both measure several different types of changes – which is why the lie-detector is called a polygraph, from the Greek meaning 'many'. Neither are very accurate by themselves and require supplementing by other methods.

Concealing defensiveness and disagreement are not the same as lying, yet both involve an outward expression which is at variance with the inner state of the mind. It is this tension which causes the observable behaviours in both cases. Traditional moralists describe lying as *loquatio contra mentem* – speaking contrary to the mind. That seems a good definition for both.

LIGHTNING REMINDER

★ *Agreement and disagreement, liking and not liking, are clearly signalled by NVC.*

★ *The persuasion player can induce positive feelings by subtle, graded use of NVC.*

★ *NVC will tell you when the feelings differ from the words.*

NVC AND APPEARANCE

Appearance is an aspect of NVC which can be prepared in advance; it can be quite powerful, as the account in the last chapter of the man crossing against the lights in different kinds of clothing showed. Even one's natural physical appearance can be modified to give desirable cues.

The appearance of the body

Attractiveness can be enhanced in many ways, from plastic surgery to good skin care and grooming. Height can be modified by high heels, platform soles and carefully chosen clothes. And such factors are important because they relate to stereotype programs held in the brain. Thin and bony people tend to be seen as quiet and tense; fat people as warm-hearted and dependent; muscular people as adventurous and self-reliant; tall people as intelligent. These judgements can sometimes loosely accord with the facts of the personality, but you need to be on your guard to avoid reacting in line with programs which are not, taken alone, very accurate.

People who wear spectacles are often seen as intelligent. This was dramatically demonstrated when it was discovered that, on first meeting, a person wearing spectacles would be credited with 14 more IQ points than someone without spectacles. (IQ measurement is a standard scoring of conventional intelligence in which 100 = average.) However, after five minutes of conversation this effect had worn off.

Hair is another controllable factor – length, style, colour, wig. Long hair in men is associated with a defiant attitude towards society and may, in practice, exclude one from a wide range of employment. Hair, including facial hair, also has sexual overtones.

Hair can often give clues to our psychological state. Marriage counsellors sometimes notice that a distressed wife has lank, even greasy, hair. As her psychological condition improves so does her hair condition.

> *When my cousin first grew a beard he found that it had a marked effect on the women he knew. Some reacted with disgust, while others became distinctly more cuddly. However his wife approved of his new appearance; she said it was like committing adultery without all the hassle. So the beard stayed on.*

Clothes as identifiers

As well as enhancing appearance, clothes and accessories act as identifiers. In many societies (including our own in earlier periods of history) clothes are used to identify social class by quite formal standards. The distinctions are often protected by strong conventions. In Western society today the distinctions are more informal and, with the increase in mass-produced high quality clothing, no longer so clear. But they still exist. Couture clothing will indicate at least wealth (which may nowadays equate to social position), and many people can recognise the cost of clothes from the cut and the cloth. Men's suits are commonly off-the-peg, but sometimes imitate the hand-made article by the stitching on the lapel.

Sufficiently high status enables one to break these rules. For instance, a successful or wealthy woman may boast that her dress is from a cheap chain store. But it may be accompanied by understated, expensive accessories. And older men will often be seen in sports jackets which are well past their wear-by-date. If they are mistaken by an insensitive caller for the gardener the anecdote becomes a matter of pride.

A friend of mine called at a distinguished merchant bank in order to negotiate an industrial loan of several hundred million pounds. He was wearing a barathea overcoat of an extremely expensive type. When he mentioned that this had been bought from a charity shop for £10 he was simply not believed. It was assumed to be some sort of complicated joke.

Clothes will identify the type of job. The phrases 'blue collar' and 'white collar' are indications of this. They will also suggest personality – from the flamboyant or eccentric to the conventional. John Major is often described as a grey man and depicted as such in a satirical puppet show. This is a combination of his perceived personality and the soberness of his suiting.

Particular grouping may be identifiable from dress, sometimes combined with other aspects of appearance. Membership of a gang may be shown in this way; similarly a tie or a fraternity pin will proclaim membership of a restricted group. Outsiders adopt these valued signs at their peril.

Clothing may also convey explicit messages: uniforms are an example of this. These can also have the quality of indicating that different rules apply. Thus the anonymity of the soldier's uniform may enable him to reduce his normal sensitivity and perform unpleasant tasks; the doctor's coat or the nurse's uniform may sanction invasions of physical and psychological privacy; the police officers' uniforms will allow you to approach them even though they are strangers to you.

Appearance and the persuasion player

Normally we create our appearance according to our self-image or the image to which we naturally aspire. Therefore the persuader will obtain many clues from careful observation. You should particularly notice discrepancies between personality and appearance since these will tell you of your opponent's aspirations and intentions.

You must, of course, be aware of the messages you are transmitting through your own self-presentation, and you should tailor this to fit your strategy.

TERRITORY

Territory is important to human beings and appears to be a very ancient instinct. An obvious aspect, which I have already touched on, is our sensitivity to the invasion of our personal space. We are surrounded by a kind of psychological oval into which we do not like people to come, unless we are intimate with them. However we are prepared to break the rule in certain circumstances – for instance, in a crowded lift or crowded train. But here we avoid eye contact in order to show that the closeness has no meaning. Interestingly we seem to have extended this personal space to the motor car. We feel indignant if the car behind us comes too close and our indignation often outweighs the danger involved. But we permit it in a traffic jam.

We can be aware of territory in restaurants or on tables in trains. As the other person's hand or baggage begins to stray into what we see as our space, our anxiety and resentment increase. If we have delineated our territory on the beach we are hostile to any trespassers.

Territory is important at work too. Size of office denotes size of territory, and the holding of territory is, in primitive terms, power. Important people are likely to have larger offices and they may site their desks well back so that any invader is made fully aware of the space they have to cross. The territory behind the desk is a holy of holies – come behind a person's desk and speak over their shoulder only if you want a row or if you are so superior that they only hold their territory by your leave. Even in open plan offices you will observe how individuals often move filing cabinets and screens so as to create territory, and then personalise it in various ways.

Home is also territory. As I pointed out in Chapter 3 we automatically defer to our host, whatever his or her status, when we are on their ground. The wise sales person, calling perhaps by appointment, stands back from the door when it is opened and waits to be asked to sit down. The salesperson may even start the conversation by some approving remark about the territory they have entered.

> *'Please make yourself at home,' is what we say to our guests. But notice how our resentment grows when they take us literally, and start using the territory and its equipment as if they really did own it. Some years ago we used to have foreign language students staying with us. But we found that a year was usually the maximum before we began to resent their territorial incursions. This was rarely the student's fault; how could they know exactly where we had drawn the line? I even feel a slight pang of territorial jealousy when one of our beloved, married children, sits on what I think is my chair in the kitchen.*

Young children are strongly territorial and tactful visiting adults stand back until the child comes to them. You know you have made progress when you are invited to visit their bedroom or their nursery. But even then you must show respect. However, children do not reciprocate; that is, they will invade our personal space and our territory without a thought. And we normally let them – presumably because of some inherited instinct of openness towards the young of the species.

LIGHTNING REMINDER

★ *Appearance conveys important NVC messages, both in the general way we look and the clothes we wear.*

★ *Effective NVC needs sensitive awareness, and use, of personal territory.*

MASTERY OF NVC

Mastery of NVC requires continual observation, study and practice. The persuasion player must never miss an opportunity to watch and practise NVC. Without fluency in this crucial language you will never be more than an amateur in the persuasion game. A suggestion I have followed with profit is to mark my diary with the letters NVC every day for several weeks in advance. It reminded me to take just five minutes to observe NVC quite deliberately. It might be in a meeting, or in a train, or at home. I would watch behaviour, attempt to interpret it, and then reflect on the signs and signals which led to that interpretation. If you think that idea would help you, get out your diary now – before turning to the next chapter.

STRATEGIES FOR NVC

- Recognise that NVC is a language you will need to master. Study can help but continuous observation and practice are the key. Learn the individual actions, but see how they work together as clusters.
- In your next persuasion encounter with someone you do not know well, practise eye contact, co-operative seating position, open gestures etc. – and observe the effect.
- Similarly, identify the NVC which tells you how your opponent is really feeling.
- Study the NVC of people you deal with regularly. Learn their particular 'dialect' so that you can interpret more accurately.

- Analyse aspects of your appearance which you can choose, as well as the clothes and accessories you wear. Do they convey the right NVC in all circumstances? Get into the habit of thinking this through when you dress in the morning – in the light of the day ahead.
- Observe how you identify your territory and how you feel about it. Experiment with invading others' territory (not while driving your motor car!) and see the reactions. Be ready to use conciliatory NVC to restore peace.
- Make long-term reminders, perhaps in your diary, for deliberate practice in observation and use of NVC.

5

Persuasion from the platform

PUBLIC SPEAKING is the key forum for the persuasion player. Because it happens in 'real time', with little opportunity for reflection, the techniques of persuasion are at their most effective. You can decide what the audience will remember and what they should forget; you can decide what your audience should feel; you can decide what your audience should decide.

MOST OF US are called to the public platform from time to time. It may be on a social occasion or perhaps at a local society. It may be a business presentation or to plead our case before a planning tribunal. It is an opportunity for persuasion in which we not only hold the complete deck of cards in our hand, but we can choose which card to play and in what order.

This chapter is not a complete guide to public speaking. I have dealt with the whole topic at length in my book. *How to Get Your Own Way in Business.* Here I will confine myself to a brief overview, with particular reference to the programs which are typically enlisted by the persuasive speaker. You may like to study this in conjunction with the section in Chapter 3 on credibility.

SPEECHES ARE ONLY HEARD ONCE

Speeches are a different form of communication from either written material or conversation. We can read written material at our own pace and re-read and study at our leisure. In conversation we can question the speaker to test the truth of what he is saying or ask him to clarify or develop it. But, when we listen to a speech, we can only hear what the speaker chooses to say, and at the pace at which he chooses to say it.

This characteristic makes the speech a very valuable method of persuasion. By the end of an effective speech the audience will be left with the right impressions and the right feelings, while remembering little of what has actually been said – and with almost no opportunity to exercise their critical faculties upon it.

> *Remember the story of the man who asked his friend, a great orator, to write the speech he must make at his trial. Initially he liked the speech but, by the third time of reading, he was complaining that it simply did not stand up to examination. His friend replied, 'You quite forget that the judges are to hear it only once.'*

LOSS OF MEMORY

As a speaker, your ability to control what your audience will remember and what they will forget requires you to capitalise on the specialised program the brain uses for coping effectively with memory. It has to deal with masses of information – but only some of this needs to be retained for more than a few seconds. So the brain has a short-term memory, of very limited capacity. As soon as it overflows the earlier information is lost.

But, before it goes, we are able to transfer this information into long-term memory by use of a number of devices. Perhaps the simplest example is that of repetition. When listening to a speech the degree to which we transfer to long-term memory – or the items which we transfer – is largely under the control of the speaker. In effect the speaker can cover a subject comprehensively while deciding what we will actually remember. It is a very real power. In this chapter you will see many examples of this.

SETTING YOUR OBJECTIVES

An essential preliminary to speech preparation is setting out objectives. That sounds obvious but it is only too easy to miss out this stage. Take this objective as an example:

> *'I want to explain to the committee just why the erection of the proposed block of flats will spoil the look of the neighbourhood and lead to overcrowding.'*

Compare that objective with the following:

> *'I want a majority of the committee to realise and deplore the effect that the proposed block of flats will have on the look of the neighbourhood and how the overcrowding will disadvantage both the neighbours and the flat dwellers themselves – so that the committee votes down building permission.'*

The second example seems merely to be an expanded restatement of the first. But notice that it is now expressed in terms of the audience's point of view. The objective of the speech is not what *we* have to do but what change we want to bring about in the listeners. Immediately, our minds start thinking about how we can achieve this objective:

- What will be the best material to select?
- How will we engage the listeners' emotions?
- In what order should we put our material to give it the biggest impact?
- How will we deal with the objections to our case which will be in the audience's minds?
- And so on. In answering these questions we will find not only that the speech has already been largely constructed, but that we have also given ourselves a criterion by which to judge exactly what it should contain.

So, as an accomplished speaker you must start your preparation by asking a first question: 'How do I want my audience to change in between the time that I stand up and the time I sit down?' If you can answer that question you are well on the way to success; if you can't, failure should come as no surprise.

Purpose, Price and Probability

With your objectives clearly in mind apply the Motivation Triangle. How will your speech meet the Purposes of your audience, including its hidden agendas? How can you present the Price they will have to pay so that it seems worth while? Will you leave them confident that their purposes will be achieved?

FIRST IMPRESSIONS

On no occasion are first impressions more important than at the beginning of a speech. What are the right first impressions to make?

- This speaker has something interesting to say; I am going to want to listen to her.

- I like this speaker. I feel she is talking to me.

- This is a speaker with authority; she knows what she's talking about.

Imagine a speaker who did not show those characteristics. How much attention would you give him or her; would you be likely to be swayed by the arguments? And, being a first impression, the view you take in the first minute or two will colour the whole speech.

If you have done your work well in defining objectives you should have no difficulty in establishing that you have something interesting to say. Here are some examples of phrases which you might use early in a speech:

We have all admired the plans and the architect's impression of how the new block will look. But I want to suggest to you that, should it be built, it will prove a white elephant within three years. And I want to tell you why I think so.

Here you establish that you are reasonable, quite prepared to pay compliments where they are due. So the use of the dramatic phrase 'white elephant' pulls up the hearers with a start — they can almost see the headline in the local newspaper. It has them worried. They are going to want to know the speaker's reasons, aren't they?

I get two or three letters a week from my constituents complaining about planning decisions. That doesn't surprise me — we can't please all of the people all of the time. But I'm not looking to double or treble my postbag. Are you? Yet if we approve this application that's exactly what will happen. Let me explain why.

This is a direct appeal to the committee members' self-interest. First, they certainly don't want to increase their complaint mail; but, more important, votes at the next election might depend on this decision. Notice in that example how our speaker has chosen to emphasise his similarity to the audience

– they are all in the same boat. Similarity, as we saw in Chapter 3, is a way of achieving credibility.

I was taking an evening stroll up by Hill Side yesterday evening – with the dog. The sun was just setting; it was really beautiful. Then, into my mind's eye, came the picture of this new block we're considering. I saw it silhouetted gauntly against the sky. And I have to tell you I shuddered.

See how this appeals to the imagination. We can identify with the speaker and, in doing so, we almost feel the shudder in ourselves. We are captured, we want to know more.

There are many different ways of interesting an audience; these are just examples. The best test you can use is to ask yourself whether your chosen way would interest *you* enough to want to listen.

MAKING CONTACT

Each member of the audience wants to feel that you are talking to them. The main weapon you have here is your eyes. Looking at your audience, allowing your eyes to rove over them, defines who you are speaking to. Each person will have felt that they have caught your eye at least once and are thus personally engaged in a dialogue with you.

The use of the eyes is part of projection, and it is quite difficult to look at your audience in this way without using complementary posture movements and throwing your voice out to your listeners. Volume of voice is not as important as consciously feeling that you are talking to everyone, including those at the fringes. Your desire to address all your audience in a personal way will ensure projection, and retain the natural flexibility and variety in your voice.

> *A very experienced speaker, a deacon in his local church,
> was taken aback at a conference when the auditorium
> lights were lowered. 'How could I see my audience?' The
> advice he received was to look around his whole
> audience before the lights went down and then to gaze
> out at the picture in his memory. He can't see the
> audience but they can see him. He was also reminded
> that listening to the subtle noises of an audience is even
> more important under such circumstances.*

NB: If you are using a microphone, always test it beforehand.
It is too late, once you have actually started your speech, to find
that you don't know how to switch it on, or that the sound level
is wrong, or that it whistles.

STRUCTURE – YOU KNOW WHAT YOU ARE TALKING ABOUT

And of course you do because you have clear objectives and a
strategy for achieving them. This alone gives you the
confidence that enables dominance signals to come naturally to
you (see Chapter 3). But you will also have a clear structure to
your speech and it will usually be right to let your audience
know what this is going to be:

> *To help us think about this application I want first to say
> something about how its appearance fits in with area, then
> on what effects that number of new residents will have on
> their neighbours' convenience and, finally, on what many
> of our constituents have already said to me about the
> proposal.*

By speaking in this way, not only will you have demonstrated that you know what you're talking about, you will also have ensured that they know what you're talking about and will be able to follow the course of the argument easily.

In this example the speaker's qualifications would be well known to the listeners; in other circumstances the speaker might have taken the opportunity to mention them.

Clear and simple structure is important: clear, because audiences need to have things spelt out for them – they need to know where they are in a speech and how it fits into the argument; simple, because, however intelligent the individuals may be, audiences tend to be thick. They will not know what to attend to, or even what conclusions to draw, unless you indicate this to them. No speech should contain more than three or four main points – and even those will sometimes be too many. And never exceed 20 minutes, unless you are very, very good. Audience retention goes down after 20 minutes, and even into reverse after half an hour. The long-term memory will have been overloaded by too much information in too short a time.

The old advice, 'Tell them what you're going to tell them, tell them, then tell them you've told them', remains good. It enables you to give the material three times, in different forms – thus using repetition to ensure that your main points are well into the long-term memory.

Order is vital

The order in which you speak about items should always be considered. Do you want to lull them into a sense of comfort before hitting them with a powerful contrary argument? Should you get them on your side at the beginning with some powerful points or leave this until nearer the end? Do you want to gain your effect by piling argument upon argument until there is no room for doubt in their minds? Different speeches require different ordering of material; but you always have to think about which order is likely to be most effective for each particular case.

THE BEGINNING AND THE END

The opening is important because of first impressions; the closing is just as important because of the prominence program. The last points that you make stick in the mind precisely because they are the most recent. And it's following those last points that you want action – in this case, their votes. Notice how the speaker in the example which follows actually spells out for the audience what they should think and what they should do. Nevertheless the speaker phrases it carefully to avoid any sense of pressure which might cause the committee to react with obstinacy. (We will look more fully at the reactance program in Chapter 8.)

So, we've seen how the architecture of this new block is quite out of character with the houses on Hill Rise, and how it ruins the skyline. We've noticed how the additional residents will increase the traffic flow and the noise in that quiet area to an unacceptable degree. And we know that many of our constituents are so angry about it that they're building a pressure group. It shows how strongly people feel. We can only conclude that this development is quite unsatisfactory, and therefore I invite you to turn it down.

LIGHTNING REMINDER

★ *Public speaking is powerful because you can control whether or not the long-term memory is used.*

★ *You must be clear about how you want your audience to change (objectives). Remember the Motivation Triangle.*

★ *Use a clear and simple structure; three or four points are quite enough.*

★ *Grab them with your opening; grab them with*
your closing; and remember that order is
always important.

HOW TO PRESENT YOUR CASE

When you are speaking you need to think about your audience's programs just as you will think about the programs of an individual whom you wish to persuade. You need to know how your audience is likely to be thinking about the question before you start and what issues are going to be difficult – and thus important to cover. You will also need to know about individuals or groups within the audience who will have special interests or contrary views; then you can decide how to address these. In our example we will assume that the speaker has decided that the effect on the constituents is the point most likely to motivate the committee. That's what they really care about.

Our speaker has, of course, to deal with the rational case – aesthetics and population density – because the committee will need to have apparently respectable reasons for making their decision. The psychological accounting program is active here. But the speaker signals right at the beginning that he is going to deal with constituents' reactions, and he wisely chooses to make this the last point in his closing words. In that way, using the prominence program, he elevates his last point into first place in the audience's minds.

CONTROLLING THE MEMORY

With an idea of how you are going to start and finish, you are ready to build up the central part of your speech. A number of factors will apply – though not all of them will apply to each speech.

Helping them to forget

Imagine a sagging washing line. That curve is rather like the attention pattern of an audience: high at the beginning and the end; lower in the middle. This has often been checked – by measuring heartbeat rate or by the parts of a speech from which most items are recalled. The speaker in our example might want to make use of this. Supposing he is aware that some members of the committee are anxious to increase the number of council tax payers and that this will lead some of the committee to favour the building application. You have to deal with that objection because it's important enough. And you remember the contribution that facing up to an objection makes to credibility (Chapter 3). But you don't want to give it prominence. So you deal with it somewhere in the middle of your speech when it will gain the least attention. Moreover, you follow it immediately by a fact of some importance – giving the listeners no time to reflect on what has been said.

> *Of course such a block of flats will increase the number of council tax payers in the borough and that's very important to all of us. But in this case it's likely to give us only a short-term advantage – and there's a price to pay. If we always yield to the temptation of increasing population density one day we'll be as crowded as an inner city borough – and look at the problems they have in raising council tax! And, talking of population density, have you thought about how all those extra cars are going to exit from Hill Rise? I've calculated that ...*

The listeners should be left with the impression that you've dealt with the problem, even if they can't remember exactly how.

Helping them to remember

But most often your concern will be to keep the audience's attention and recall high because you have some important things to say. Here are some useful techniques.

- Use **variety in your voice.** You can change the pitch, the volume and the speed. Remember that the human system is built to be alerted by change (Chapter 1).
- Use **variety in your presentational method.** For example, you might ask your listeners to read a hand-out to show how population density will increase if the flats are built. The primary purpose here is to regain the audience's attention by a change of method. On other occasions you might want to use a slide or an overhead projector, or you might ask the audience a question. You will notice how your audience wakes up every time you introduce such a change.

  Like the microphone, other mechanical aids must be checked beforehand. Rehearse them and, if you are using borrowed equipment, make sure you have a run through first. Experienced speakers carry a small pack of drawing pins, Blu-Tak, paper clips, board markers that are known to work, spirit pens, spare transparencies for overhead projectors etc. This is one occasion when the deepest pessimism is justified.

- We have noticed the use of **repetition;** it can be employed directly for driving a point home and into the long-term memory:

  Building this block of flats will not just double the traffic in Hill Rise, it will treble it. Let me repeat that: three times as many cars in that quiet, leafy road.

- **Pauses** are invaluable. They give the listener at least a microsecond in which to consolidate the point being made and one or two longer pauses can add dramatic emphasis. The audience's recall is hindered by a delivery which is too slow – the beginning of the thought has been expunged from the short-term memory before it is complete; but it is helped by a moderately quick delivery which allows pauses for immediate reflection.

  Just as you can use a pause to emphasise a point so you will avoid a pause if you prefer the point to be immediately forgotten. Indeed, as in the council tax objection above, you may quickly insert attention-grabbing material to reinforce your strategy.

- Used sparingly, and in accordance with your personality and the nature of the speech, a little **dramatic effect** can be helpful.

  So what I say is that an increase in the population of Hill Rise is quite unacceptable. (Tears up population density hand-out, and scatters on the floor.)

  Less vigorous but often effective is a memorable pause, for example:

  Do we want to set up a slum in the suburbs?

- Do you think that phrase might remain in the mind long after the speech is over?
- Sometimes a physical object can be used; this can be effective because it's unusual. Here, for example, you might take some children's bricks and place four in a row, pause – and then add two more on top of one of the bricks, saying:

  Is that the sort of skyline we really want?

- Ingenuity may be called for. Suppose that among your objections to the new flats is the fact that the quality of the sound insulation in the building will be poor. You might play a brief tape recording of a late night party. Of course it proves nothing, but it's different. And, incidentally, it brings to prominence in everyone's mind the thought that intrusive noise late at night is painful and infuriating.
- But use your discretion with anything that might be seen as a gimmick. Reserve such ideas for the occasions when you really need them.

THE USE OF HUMOUR

Humour is a useful aid for a speaker. It can draw the audience together into a group, and it makes the speaker more likeable, and therefore more credible. It is valuable for variety because it helps the audience to relax and provides them with a contrast to the meat of the speech. But if you are not a humorist, don't use it – there are plenty of other techniques to gain your ends. If you are, don't overdo it. Too much humour means that the jokes are remembered and the speech is forgotten. Remember that humour, as well as everything else, must serve the objectives you have set yourself. Plan your humour. You might, for example, want to use some at the beginning while you are establishing yourself with the group, followed by one or two points later on – perhaps where you need to leaven a dull passage or when you want to prevent your audience committing the last point you made to their long-term memory.

GETTING YOUR POINT ACROSS

You will often find yourself faced by the challenge of getting a complex point across to your audience. And it is a challenge because of an audience's reduced capacity to understand and recall. Here, the characteristics of a speech – with which I opened this chapter – are working against you. Here are some ideas.

Visual aids

Visual aids can often help to communicate complex ideas. For example, a graph showing rising population in the borough will make more impression on most minds than a list of figures. Visual aids can also be used to demonstrate the main points of an idea while you are speaking about it. Or you can use them as reminder points to consolidate long-term memory.

A large insurance company was in the habit of congratulating itself on its steadily rising business. Then one executive prepared a chart which adjusted increases for inflation. For the first time the company actually accepted what they had really known all along. Allowing for inflation their business had actually been decreasing. But they had to see the picture before they could believe the words.

Avoid the mistake of crowding visual aids. Every item should be easy to see and, if you are using written points, then eight lines is about the maximum. An illegible or confused visual aid is worse than no visual aid at all. And always explain them:

The vertical scale on the left shows the number of tens of thousands of population in the borough; the horizontal scale shows time, starting in 1980. You can see how population scarcely increased until 1987, then there was a steep jump − and it's continued to rise ever since.

Once again you are guiding the audience's thought processes; they won't do it for themselves.

Statement − example − restatement

Think about the formula: statement − example − restatement. Here it is in action.

- **Statement** 'As a committee we have always been dedicated to improving the quality of life for all the residents in the borough. We don't want to change that principle now.'

- **Example** 'Only six months ago we vetoed the Lancaster Road development because we thought it inappropriate.

And we thought it worthwhile to spend a large sum on public swimming facilities.'

- **Restatement** 'So we have an excellent record for keeping the borough a good place to live in. This decision gives us an opportunity to show we still think that way.'

Statement – example – restatement, gives us the advantage of repetition; and the use of the example not only clarifies exactly what we mean, it also brings it to life in a vivid way. The formula maximises the chances of the statement being properly understood, but also gives it motivational force – and drives it into the long-term memory.

Stories

Stories are an important weapon in the armoury of the speaker, because they address the understanding of the imagination. As we saw in Chapter 3, they can often have more impact than the plain, dry facts. The story about taking the dog for an evening walk on Hill Rise, which was given as an example of opening a speech, demonstrates the power of the story. Use stories frequently.

Incidentally, stories are another way of introducing variety into a speech. They always engage our interest.

Analogies

Analogies are like mental stepping stones. They help the audience to get their minds across to a new idea by means of an idea which is already familiar. Here are some examples.

Of course we are all aware of the government's policy for building more housing units. And we want to respond to that. But we have to be prudent. It's like deciding what size you want your family to be. You may love children but you have to balance increasing your family size against the needs of its existing members. That's the sort of decision we're making today.

*I realise the specifications for this new block are within the
building regulations. But, taken all in all, the quality is
low..Do you walk into a shop and always choose the very
cheapest brand? Or do you take the view that it's better in
the long run to go for quality? What's this block going to
look like in 20 or 30 years' time?*

Consistency is the program at work here. If we behave in a
certain way in our private lives it seems inconsistent to behave
differently in our public decisions. Not all analogies turn out to
be valid on analysis; but who has time to analyse in the middle
of a speech?

PERSUASION PROGRAMS

This simple overview of the construction of a speech has
already incorporated a number of programs. But virtually
every program we discuss in this book can be used in a speech
– and used with strong effect since the audience has only the
time which the speaker allows it to spot the program and
mount defences. Let's take a few examples at random.

- The speaker is well groomed and has a pleasant manner.
  (*attractiveness = credibility*)
- 'We've got to accept that with flats at this size and price the
  borough is going to attract more one-parent families. We're
  going to have to absorb all the social problems that come
  with that.' (*stereotyping*)
- 'It's not that long ago that boroughs like ours were building
  tower blocks and increasing population like forest fires.
  Look at the outcome of that. Maybe we should be paying
  more attention to the new approach that many boroughs are
  now adopting, including ones next door to us. They are all
  going for quality rather than quantity.' (*both the dangers*

and the advantages of the herd instinct in the same argument)

- The use of words or phrases which carry pleasant or unpleasant associations according to the speaker's need – such as 'gauntly', 'inner city boroughs', 'quiet leafy road', 'slum', 'cheapest brand'. (*language program*)

LIGHTNING REMINDER

★ *Your audience will have its personal programs; address them.*

★ *Help your audience to forget by preventing them from using their long-term memory.*

★ *Help your audience to remember by using pauses, repetition and dramatic prominence.*

★ *Humour can be valuable; but only if it comes naturally.*

★ *Speeches make complex explanations difficult; use the right techniques.*

★ *Don't forget to use all the programs you need.*

★ *Rehearse and check all your equipment. Trust no one.*

PREPARATION AND REHEARSAL

With clear objectives, an opening, an ending and a well-planned centre section, it is time to prepare for the actual delivery of the speech. And here many people encounter a difficulty. They are nervous about speaking from notes; what they really feel they need is a script. But, unless you speak directly to an audience, you will lack all the force and persuasiveness which comes from the direct contact between the speaker and the audience. Indeed, why be there at all? You might just as easily send a tape recording or a script which can be read out loud in your absence.

> *In ordinary conversation the mind is working at two levels. One level is doing the speaking and listening, the other is analysing and planning what to say next. On the platform the second level can be paralysed by nervousness − it just goes blank.*
>
> *Good speech preparation and rehearsal can help; so can the availability of back-up notes that will not let you down. But the long-term answer is practice. Once you know you are capable of giving good speeches, your nerves will recede. But you will never lose them altogether.*

Let's look at a technique which has helped many people.

Preparation technique

Stage 1

Lock yourself into a private room and on a sheet of paper write down the main headings of the structure you have planned, leaving room between each heading. Then start giving your speech out loud to an imaginary audience. I like to stand up behind a chair to give me the right atmosphere. As you finish each section, pause and scribble in simple notes of what you have said. Sometimes only a word or two will be enough. When you have gone right through the speech, section by section, start from the beginning again − giving the whole speech once more, in your own words. You may want to add or subtract notes as you go.

Stage 2

When, following further rehearsal, you feel reasonably happy with the material, time the speech − trying as far as possible to give the material at the speed you will actually use. You may find that this obliges you to prune back − speeches are often too long, rarely too short.

Stage 3

You now have notes for a speech which you are capable of giving in your own words. Lots more rehearsal is required − to get variety, to judge pauses, to build in gesture or movement, to introduce visual aids − and all the elements which turn a dry account into a living and effective performance. As you do so, try to cut down on your notes so that, in the end, they are no more than a reminder in case of need.

Stage 4

Have a rehearsal in front of a friend or a member of your family. This is much more nerve-racking than actually giving the speech to an audience; and that's the main reason. It's like the dress rehearsal for a play − you have the chance to practise giving your material in very stressful circumstances. This is when you drop your notes, lose your slides and get a coughing fit at the worst possible moment. The actual performance will be smooth as silk by comparison.

Your friend will be able to comment on your material and your delivery. Don't necessarily accept their advice, but remember that they, like your audience, are hearing the speech for the first time, and so their immediate reactions are likely to be a good guide.

Stage 5

Always have a final run through to yourself on the day you are making the speech. This helps to ensure that what you are planning to say is in the forefront of your memory.

If the prospect of relying on notes alone is still too daunting, the next best method is to go back to Stage 3, when you have a complete speech ready in your own words. Tape the speech as you rehearse it and then transcribe it into a script. Transcribe literally, faults and all. Spoken patterns are different from written patterns and it is the former you want to retain. Mark up key words in your script with a highlighting crayon – perhaps in one colour for structural points and another for minor points. Continue rehearsing – using the script as little as you can, but knowing that it is always available should your memory lock. Pay particular attention to keeping your gaze on the audience as much as possible; and, when you rehearse, have this checked.

All this may sound like a great deal of hard work. It is. Many hours of preparation and rehearsal may be needed for quite a short speech – even when you are fairly experienced. You are making the very best use of an opportunity to persuade a number of people and using all the most powerful cards in the persuasion game. And you are addressing your audience from the heart – with spontaneity. How can you hope to do that without a great deal of preparation?

LIGHTNING REMINDER

★ *Powerful public speaking means addressing the audience directly.*

★ *Follow a simple routine to develop a spoken rather than a written speech which only needs notes.*

★ *If you have to use a script read them a speech and not a dissertation.*

STRATEGIES FOR PERSUASION FROM THE PLATFORM

- Speeches are for moving minds. Before you start write down the answer to the question: 'How do I want my audience to change in between the time that I stand up and the time that I sit down?' You may have more than one objective.
- Conduct your motivation analysis, using Purpose, Price and Probability.
- Ponder on your objectives until you have found a clear and simple structure for your speech that will satisfy the Motivation Triangle. The simpler the better.
- The first key point is the opening.
  - Grasp their attention by drama, or by worrying them, or by posing a question they want answered, or by appealing to the imagination.
  - Make your credentials clear.
  - Spell out your structure.
  - Encompass them with your roving gaze.
- The second key point is the close.
  - Tell them what you've told them.
  - Leave them with the real message ringing in their ears.
- Consider the order of items. Where will you deal with objections to your case? How can you make sure they remember and forget just what you want them to? Review the ideas in this chapter to give your speech emphasis, variety and the power to grab their attention.
- Be aware of your audience's programs; and be aware of the programs you can build into your material.
- Take special care with complex material; study the methods of communicating this.
- Develop your speech by practising out loud, using reminder notes and plenty of rehearsal. If you have to use a script let it be a transcription of your spoken speech.

Persuasion at work

6

Getting that job

THERE ARE MANY excellent books around to guide the job seeker. Their objective is to enable applicants to provide fair pictures of themselves so that they have the best chance of ending up in a job which is suited to their capacity. This chapter approaches the problem from the angle of the skilled persuader. It will tell you what really counts in the selection interview and how to make sure that you, and not the interviewer, decide the outcome.

HOW MUCH DO YOU KNOW ABOUT SELECTION INTERVIEWS?

Here's a quiz to find out. Check your answers against the information in this chapter.

1. In nearly every case firms use a selection routine involving an application form and a personal interview. Is this method of selection:

    Very reliable? Reasonably reliable? Virtually useless?

2. If a firm dropped the interview and relied on the application form, would this be likely to:

    Improve selection quality? Reduce selection quality? No difference?

3. When is the interviewer most likely to decide whether or not you will get the job?

    Towards the end of the interview? After the interview? In the first five minutes of the interview?

4. Why do interviewers like interviewing:

    To make the best choice? Nothing else to do? Makes them feel important?

5. When should you ask the questions which will tell you what you really want to know about the job:

    Before the interview? During the interview? After you've been offered the job?

THE SELECTION INTERVIEW

Interviews are conducted because neither employer nor applicant feels comfortable without the social exchange and social assessment which only an interview provides. Of course the stated purpose of the interview is to enable the employer to select the candidate who is most likely to succeed in the job. However, the evidence shows that the interview is almost entirely useless for this purpose. While trained interviewers who follow a structured interviewing path may do a little better than chance in predicting future success, the odds are firmly against an applicant ever meeting one.

On a score from 0 to 10, where 0 equates to using a pin and 10 means 100 per cent accurate predictions, the selection interview – as shown by numerous studies – scores between 1 and 2.

This knowledge is very freeing. It allows you, the skilled persuader, to forget about the careful presentation of information in order to help the interviewer to make their selection. You can concentrate primarily on conforming to the brain programs of the interviewer in order to ensure that you maximise the chance of getting a job offer.

That is the purpose of the process from the applicant's point of view. It is not to get a job, but to get a job offer. Or rather, it is to get as many job offers as you can. The process of selection is in fact carried out by the candidate rather than by the interviewer. Although you will not waste your time applying for jobs which are quite unsuitable for you, the time to decide whether you want the job comes after you have been offered it and not before. If you only get one job offer you are free to accept or reject; if you reject it you will at least benefit from the confidence which comes from knowing you are employable. If you get more than one you are free to make choices by comparison, and you will not be tempted to rationalise your decision because it is the only possibility open to you.

Inexperienced house-hunters will often fall in love with the first house that seems to fit their specifications. In no time at all they are visualising furniture and colour schemes, weaving mental patterns about their future in this inviting nest. The more experienced will look for at least three houses which attract them. They know it gives them a better picture of the available market and the choice allows them to compare a whole range of factors to inform their decision. Yet choosing a house is really a small decision compared with the job that pays for the house.

That advice may not seem helpful to someone seeking a job in a tough market where even a single job offer is a triumph. But it's an essential attitude of mind to cultivate – part of your **LIPS** (see page 53). Which applicant would *you* be more interested in taking on – someone whom no one else will employ or someone who is good enough to get a job elsewhere?

So getting a job offer is a game in which the advantage is interestingly balanced. The prospective employer has the job in their gift, and you haven't. But the prospective employer thinks they are going to make an accurate decision about your potential, and they aren't.

You want the job offer so that you can decide whether you want the job and you have the skills to ensure that your presentation gives you the best chance of being recognised as the person for the job. Who wins?

Let's review the skills you need to make sure it's you.

THE LAW OF FIRST IMPRESSIONS

The law of first impressions, which we have already seen, states that we construct a mental picture of people when we first meet them, and then tend to preserve that picture as long as we can by noticing any evidence which supports it, and by ignoring any evidence which contradicts it. Of all the brain programs we have looked at, the program of first impressions is likely to be used most frequently by the skilled persuader and it is certainly one of the most powerful.

> *We probably developed the genes for first impressions very early in our history. The pre-humans who failed to react quickly to possible new dangers did not survive to breed. Those who did, and stuck to their decision without dithering, lived to breed another day. Guess which ones we are likely to be descended from!*

As we saw in Chapter 1, the senses, brain and nervous system are all physically adapted to notice change and comparison because change means opportunity or danger. The whole dynamic of our physiology is structured towards forming first impressions from scant evidence and acting upon them. This characteristic, undoubtedly useful in the jungle, can lead us astray today. So, managing the first impressions made on others, as well as being on our guard against the first impressions made on us, can be important.

The selection routine is a classic game of first impression management. A decision which may last a lifetime is taken on the basis of an application form and an interview. There are no second impressions until it's too late.

A selection interview may take no longer than half an hour; but even this may be far too long. A study of personnel selection in the Canadian army showed that the minds of most interviewers were made up after the first four minutes, usually on irrelevant information.

LIGHTNING REMINDER

★ *Selection interviews are a very unreliable way of picking people – but you can capitalise on this.*

★ *The object is to get job offers; your selection comes later.*

★ *Concentrate on the first impressions program; it's vital for interviews.*

THE APPLICATION FORM OR CURRICULUM VITAE (CV)

The application form sets out the headings with spaces to indicate the information which is required. The CV allows you to choose your own structure and information, since you write it yourself. (See *Useful Reading* for information on the usual headings.) Either would normally be sent with a covering letter. Your CV should be kept on a word processor if possible, because it is in fact tailored for each job you are applying for, although this is not obvious from its appearance.

The purpose of the application form or CV

The purpose of the application form is not to get you the job but to get you the interview. This is lucky because the evidence suggests that if the prospective employer were confined to a well-planned application form, and avoided the interview altogether, the predictions would be more accurate. Fortunately for the skilled persuader, custom and instinct will make the prospective employer want to conduct an interview, and thus unwisely to invite you on to a playing field where you have all the advantages.

I do not mean that the application form is irrelevant to the interview. It gives content and structure — for the most part chosen by the applicant in order to get the right questions asked. Nor do I mean that the application should in any way be untruthful; skilled presentation relies on selection and care of expression, not mendacity, for its success. What I do mean is that if you don't get the application form right, you won't get an interview.

The ideal application is one which demonstrates that you have the necessary qualifications and experience for the job, and which leaves the reader wanting to know more.

Remember that first impressions apply to the application form itself. Unless the nature of the form requires you to, restrict the personal details at the head to essentials. You can put the rest in later. Immediately under this summarise your CV in a single sentence, e.g. 'A senior brand manager with a demonstrable success record in a variety of retail consumer goods'.

It should stand out, even if only ever so slightly, from the pile of other applications on the desk. It should have a feel about it that makes the interviewer think: 'That's a candidate I'm going to enjoy seeing'. Thus the first, first impression is made.

The evidence suggests that to include some negative information about yourself establishes the credibility of your application (see Chapter 3). Your drawback should be selected with care. 'I am not fluent in foreign languages' might do if the firm in question has no dealings with foreigners; 'Can read French and German, but only fluent in German' would be better for an import/export firm.

You may not falsely boost your qualifications but you may omit them. If you are obviously overqualified for the job an employer is likely to wonder why you have failed to get a job elsewhere, and will suspect that you will leave them for a more suitable job as soon as you have the opportunity.

If you know someone in good standing at the company where you are making the application you have a great advantage, through using the endorsement program. Not only can you find out more about the job and the culture biases which apply, but you can also get just the push you need. Your acquaintance does not have to recommend you; just to say that a friend is interested in the job and that your acquaintance advised you to apply in the usual way. In the right ear, this will ensure that your application gets through the first hurdle. You should, of course, briefly mention in your covering letter that you know this person, so that the link is made.

Work your way through the questions, or the headings in the form, initially in rough. Consider in each case how to phrase the answer so that it conforms or tends towards the job requirement. But make sure you will be able to answer the supplementary questions your information provokes. Work experience will be crucial and many young applicants have obtained posts on the strength of holiday jobs alone. Positions of responsibility in voluntary organisations which indicate social skills and reliability can be equally valuable.

Catherine was applying, with many others, for a trainee post as a merchant banker. She was able to point out that she had managed ice-cream vans during university vacations. She did not feel obliged to add that this had only been for two days while her employer was taking a long weekend. She got the job because the other candidates had no management experience.

Hobbies and recreations should be selected according to whether you are genuinely interested and can talk about them, and whether they tend to confirm, or at least not contradict, your qualifications. Interviewers often choose to start with this section in their attempt to relax you; so try to include one intriguing interest with which you can make a good start. Beware of hobbies or sports which might suggest that you would be more interested in pursuing them than doing the job itself. The whole way through ask yourself: what would I think of this answer if I were deciding whether to see this applicant or not?

Anxiety can lead candidates to put in every possible detail which might be to their advantage. The result is a cramped form, often accompanied by pages of notes. No one reads this. A better tactic is to spot and include only the key points the interviewer is looking for. Full details are undesirable – entice the interviewer to ask you the questions you will be ready to answer.

Keep your answers brief, consistent with covering the ground. A tedious application suggests a tedious person and, like good sermons, the most effective messages are short. The same applies to the covering letter. The purpose here is not to sell yourself, but to include one further piece of relevant information, not mentioned on the application, which will make you stand out from the crowd. It may be that you have always bought the firm's product, or that your second cousin once worked for them, or that you've heard that they like to develop their employees (if you have), or you may have a special reason why you could do the job well. Remember that, like the p.s. at the bottom of a sales letter, isolated information carries more weight – it uses the prominence program described in Chapter 1.

You may have an in-built advantage, which in recent times has become rarer, of being able to spell correctly and write grammatically. This alone will put you ahead of many other candidates. If these refinements were overlooked in your education, get help before you write out your fair copy. Your handwriting should be firm, legible and clear.

LIGHTNING REMINDER

★ *The object of the job application or CV is to get you the interview; compose it on that basis.*

★ *Keep it brief and phrase it to meet the job requirement. Think of the questions you want to be asked.*

★ *Use the covering letter to make a point which will grab the attention. If you have an introduction from a contact, use it.*

THE INTERVIEWER'S PROGRAMS

You will not be surprised, having reached this stage in the book, to learn that an interviewer is not impressed by the sort of information one might expect. It might be reasonably assumed that, if you have the basic qualifications for the job (which should be already established through the application form and can be confirmed by referees), the interviewer will be judging traits and characteristics against the job specification. He won't. He will think that he is, and the questions that he asks will be apparently aimed at this, but all the evidence shows that the only really important factor is whether he likes the candidate or not. And that is the home ground of the persuasion player. Let's analyse this a little further.

• Studies of interviewers' behaviour show that while they will be clear about what characteristics are important there is little agreement between them as to what these might be. The only characteristics on which interviewers agree are evidence of social skills, and evidence of conscientiousness and reliability. Interestingly, we all tend to like people who have social skills, and we tend to trust and place reliance on people whom we like.

- The interviewer's personal programs will play a large part in their selection criteria. Among the most common are age, race and sex. These do not always work one way. For instance, while a black applicant will get a poor rating in some contexts, they may get a high rating from an interviewer pursuing a policy of favouring candidates from ethnic groups.

A doctor, interested in such matters, has recently been sending invented applications for consultancy posts at hospitals. While the details have been identical, the name has sometimes been obviously British and sometimes obviously Asian. British-named applicants were substantially more likely to be shortlisted for interview. The medical establishment is not amused.

While a woman will normally receive a lower rating for jobs in general, particularly if leadership ability is required, she will have an advantage if the job is seen as a 'feminine' one. However this bias will be less marked if she is being interviewed by a woman or if she is dressed in a more masculine fashion.

There are interviewers who believe that the answer to a single question which they always ask, or a single factor which they think pre-eminent, is enough to tell them all they need to know. All it does is to tell us about the interviewer's interviewing ability.

- Selection interviewing can be a confirmation of the interviewer's personal importance. Elsewhere in the interviewer's life he or she may be at everyone's beck and call. But right now they have the power of acceptance or rejection over a supplicant. They may not require the supplicant to be on their knees, but they do require enough deference to polish their ego.
- Appearance is an important factor; it is discussed further below.
- Non verbal communication, generally, will play a big part – for all the reasons we have already examined.
- Behaviour at the interview is taken as a good guide to usual behaviour and characteristics. In fact, the stress of an interview may well affect the behaviour of the candidate – and so give little indication of how the candidate might perform in the job itself.
- The likeability of an applicant appears to be largely a function of how similar to the interviewer the applicant is perceived to be. The program says something like: I, the interviewer, personify the company and, if I like this candidate, so will the company.
- Because of the law of first impressions the opening stages of the interview are vital. The interviewer is likely to form a fairly complete impression of a candidate in the first few minutes and to use this picture through which to interpret the rest of the interview.

> *In interviews monitored by psychologists the 'halo' effect, whereby the candidate is judged on the basis of one or two characteristics, is often seen. It may be necessary to play a tape of the interview back to convince the interviewer that they have missed important evidence which contradicts their first impressions.*

- The interviewer will be able to explain his choice as if he had objectively compared the candidate's characteristics with the demands of the job. That is, the interviewer is quite unaware of the real basis of his conclusions. He needs to rationalise the selection in order to look good to himself and others.

PREPARING FOR THE INTERVIEWER'S PROGRAMS

The first step is to find out some of the factors on which the company prides itself. For instance it may believe that it always puts the customers first or that it is at the leading edge of technology. Such concepts may have no real meaning but only exist in the collective unconscious of the company and therefore, probably, in the unconscious of the interviewer. These qualities are always, as it happens, the ones you most admire and would want to find in the company you work for.

Preparing answers

The second step is to review the information you have given in your application (you have, of course, taken a copy; persuaders routinely keep copies of all relevant documents) and consider what questions you might be asked about them; and then what supplementary questions you might be asked. In each instance you must consider what answer is most likely to imply your social skills and your reliability. Here is an example.

Interviewer: *I see you were secretary of the drama society at your university; tell me about that.*

Candidate: *Yes, it was a very interesting job. I suppose the most important part was getting people to co-operate. You know we nearly doubled our membership that year. And of course that helped our bottom line; we actually made a small profit, for the first time in years.*

In rehearsing your answers, don't forget to rehearse the modest pause which is needed to suggest that you are having to collect your thoughts in order to answer this highly original and interesting question that you hadn't anticipated. The slick answer only suggests that you are a smart alec answering an obvious question. That is not very likeable.

You should also be planning an answer or two which will indicate how well your past performance fits in with the company values for which the interviewer is subconsciously looking.

> Interviewer: *How did you enjoy working as a correspondence clerk at Snodgrass?*
>
> Candidate: *Well, I didn't very much at first. And I don't think I was very good at it. But I was lucky in my boss. She explained to me that the whole business depended on the way our customers saw us – and that the letters we wrote were often what we were judged by. Once I'd seen that, it all became worthwhile – and I really enjoyed myself.*

In one answer you have conveyed that you have faults, which makes you modest and credible; that you had a good relationship with your boss and were prepared to learn from her; that what now really interests you is good customer relations.

Your answers should be quite brief, without giving the impression that you have cut them short. The interviewer will have a low boredom threshold and needs to hear no more than a confirmation of the impression he or she has already formed.

Preparing questions

Most interviewers will reserve a few minutes to invite you to ask questions. They are aiming both to be fair and also to judge whether or not you are able to ask intelligent questions. What kind of questions do *you* like to be asked? I like questions to which I know the answer – and an answer with reflects well on me. So does the interviewer. Here is an opportunity to use some of the information you have gleaned about the company. If you have discovered that the company is rather proud of its staff benefits package, then ask whether or not they have a pension scheme. The interviewer will be delighted to answer and will certainly think you intelligent for asking such a sensible question.

Note that this is not the time to ask the questions which matter to you, such as whether promotion is slow in the company or whether it is a quick hire and fire operation. There will be plenty of time to investigate all this once you have the job offer under your belt.

Preparing your appearance

This requires emphasis. Since many jobs are won or lost within a second of entering the interviewer's office, appearance plays a big part. The style of clothes you wear will naturally depend on the nature of the job; a business suit will not always be appropriate.

> *The ideal is to look like a well turned-out member of the organisation to which you are applying. If you do so you will be recognised immediately as someone who will fit in. Your appearance says so.*

You have to show you have taken trouble. Many books advise candidates to ensure that their fingernails are clean and their shoes polished. The real point of this advice is that to neglect such details is to show the interviewer that you don't think the job is important. We all feel like this. If the person you are meeting for a first date has evidently taken no trouble about their appearance you are left to conclude either that they don't think you are worth it or that this is the best they can do even when they're trying. Neither explanation is very encouraging.

> *When I have a challenging occasion to face, like an interview, I wear the tie of my old school. It is very rarely recognised, but it makes me feel that my past friends are with me and that I carry some of the lustre of a group of whose membership I was proud. My confidence grows.*

RESPONDING TO THE INTERVIEWER'S PROGRAMS

During the interview itself you will, as we have seen, appear as someone who is socially skilled, reliable and conscientious, and sufficiently similar to the interviewer to be thoroughly likeable. You will be enthusiastic to obtain this most appealing job, and – although your self-confidence is manifest – you realise that the interviewer is an important person to whom deference is due. And you will provide the interviewer with good reasons to enable them to feel objective in their selection of you as the winning candidate.

> *Your level of deference should be carefully judged. A Uriah Heep type will not often be employed in a worthwhile position. The note should be one of respect for an important person whose decision is going to matter. But you are an important person too – though not quite so important as the interviewer.*

First impressions

Since first impressions are key, make sure you get them right. The way you open the door, the way you shake hands, the way you look the interviewer in the eye, the pleasantness of your expression and your easy smile, your respect for the interviewer's territorial space, will all contribute.

If the interviewer follows the normal pattern the first few minutes will be spent putting you at your ease. You are, of course, already at your ease – although you have conveyed the impression of slight nervousness at meeting such an important person. Respond to the interviewer's wishes and allow yourself to be put at your ease. You will know that you have succeeded when the interviewer relaxes.

Without trying to get all the information over at once, remember that the way you handle the first question or two will probably have decided the outcome of the interview. The most brilliant and apposite responses in the second half of the interview will not recover a bad beginning.

Non verbal communication

The importance of this has already been stressed. Review Chapter 4, paying particular attention to likeability and credibility, to remind yourself of the techniques you will need.

Answering questions

We have already looked at some aspects of this in preparing for the interview. Good preparation will have readied your mind for good performance, but you must avoid the danger of giving the answer to a question you had anticipated rather than to the one which was asked. It suggests that you haven't been listening and people who don't listen to us are not very likeable.

Be alive to the clues which tell you about the interviewer's personal programs. You may notice some in the way they ask questions, and the areas they explore. And, if you watch the interviewer's NVC in reaction to your answers, you will quickly pick up what interests them, so that you can build on this. Remember that, although you are a person of independent mind, you are, as it happens, rather similar to the interviewer in values and general approach to life. You may even share some interests or have had experiences in common.

Help the interviewer to talk, not only to get the program

clues, but because – as a rule of thumb – the person who talks least is most likely to win. But of course you must still come across as someone who talks easily and well; and you will need the opportunity to transmit or reinforce your key messages.

Although it is the form rather than the substance of the answers which counts, the interviewer must be left with enough objective information to justify their decision. So give it to them.

Ending the interview

Second only to first impressions are last impressions. These have a tendency to remain in the mind, because of the prominence program. Their importance will be doubled if there is another candidate to see. The immediate comparison strengthens and cements the judgement. If you are lucky enough to come immediately after and immediately before poor candidates your virtues will be framed to best advantage.

Be aware of the NVC which indicates that the interviewer is bringing the interview to a close and try to end on a high point. You might, for instance, want to reiterate your enthusiasm for the job and the company. And do not omit good eye contact when you stand up and thank the interviewer for the interview.

If you can leave the interviewer feeling the bigger and the better for the experience of interviewing you, you will have maximised your chances of success.

LIGHTNING REMINDER

★ *The interviewer's judgement will be based primarily on whether they like you – that is whether they see you as socially skilled, conscientious and reliable.*

★ *Other, standard, programs will apply; so will the interviewer's personal programs. Prepare for this but be ready to change tack if you sense you are wrong.*

★ *Give the interviewer the information they need to believe their decision is rational.*

★ *Take special care over first impressions – they may also be the last impressions.*

★ *Leave the interviewer feeling the bigger and the better for having interviewed you.*

SELECTING THE JOB

It may seem unthinkable (and your attitude of mind should indeed make it so) that, following this, you will not get a job offer. But it can happen. Because you have a built-in optimism program (see page 50) and high **LIPS,** you will not attribute this to any fundamental unworthiness in yourself. There may have been some negative circumstances in this particular case or it may be that your interviewer was lacking in perception. But the healthiest response is to review your performance and look for ways in which you can improve it for next time. People who do this tend to benefit from their experience and become more skilled at being interviewed.

When you get your job offer, you must start the process of selection. Ideally, you will be comparing it with other offers you have or are about to have. So you may need a little time. The best way to get this is to ask, once having intimated how favourably you are disposed to accepting, for an opportunity to meet some of the other people in the company, since you place such importance on knowing that you will fit in well with your peers. You will also request a few minutes to sort out one or two details you did not have time to check before – such as how to transfer your existing pension rights or whatever.

It is natural to be nervous about this; you may be anxious to formalise your agreement before it is withdrawn. But you are in fact in a very strong position. Remember the college students who committed themselves to a 7 a.m. lecture before they knew its timing (Chapter 2). Offering the job is not a legal commitment, but it is a strong psychological one. It puts you in control of the situation.

Countering your own programs

Unfortunately the successful interview will have had the effect of contaminating your own judgement. You are just as susceptible as the interviewer. In building relationships with interviewers they will have come to like you; but you will also have come to like them. And since you will feel that they personify the company you will project your view of them on to the company. The knowledge that you may never meet them again, or be working for someone different, will not protect you from this. In getting the job offer, you are flattered and impressed by the company's judgement.

The best decontaminant is to meet other members of the company. Their different personalities will give you alternative views and, although the interviewer may ask their opinion afterwards, they have much less to lose in giving you a true picture. But remember that you are also in the grip of first impressions and you may be disinclined to have your favourable impression endangered.

Make a list of the things you really want to know and note the answers down; you will be better able to evaluate them later. You will of course be checking certain facts more formally with the interviewer. Don't be a nit picker, but get the information you need; it may affect the next several years of your life.

Money

You may not have discussed a salary figure at the interview, but you will have intimated that you are looking up rather than down the scale. When you know the figure (assuming that it is not the sort of job in which salaries are non negotiable – which is much rarer than companies would have you believe), do not hesitate to ask for more if you want to. Other job offers will strengthen your resolve.

'*You know I'm very keen to take this job. but frankly I've had another offer which is a good bit more generous. I'm not necessarily expecting you to match it, because I'd much rather be with you than with them – but at the moment the gap's rather too wide. Could you suggest any way in which we could narrow it?*'

I wish I had a pound for every time that has been done to me – and with success. After all the extra money needed to secure this candidate looks very small compared with going through the whole process again, with its delay and the need to acknowledge that I will be accepting someone whom my skilled selection processes have told me is second best. But beware the counter-move:

'*Of course, you naturally want the best salary you can. I'd do the same in your position. But the fact is, on this occasion, we pretty well had to toss a coin between the three best candidates. So I think I'll need to speak to the other two first, and I'll come back to you on this if I need to.*'

You may want, at this point, to acknowledge that you are up against a persuasion player of equal skill. Only you can decide whether to call their bluff or to retract quickly. You'll both have a good laugh about it one day.

LIGHTNING REMINDER

★ *Remember, it is you who is selecting your next employers – not the other way about.*

★ *Once they have made the job offer you can ask the real questions. List what you want to know. Now is the time to bargain.*

★ *Talking informally to other employees can give you balance.*

PURPOSE, PRICE AND PROBABILITY

Purpose, Price and Profitability are, of course, playing their part in persuading the interviewer to make you a job offer. Their purpose is, in the absence of hidden agendas, to choose the best person to do the job. No problem there – though you should remember that the interviewer will want to feel that they have made a rational choice which, perhaps, they may need to justify to their superiors. Price may be a factor if there is bargaining to be done about salary and benefits; in addition the psychological cost of hiring you may be lowered if they feel that you are going to be someone pleasant to work with.

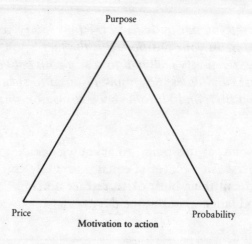

Purpose

Price   Probability
Motivation to action

Probability is usually the most important point of the triangle. How likely are you to be able to do the job and to continue doing it? We know that the most accurate way of assessing this is through an application form, which details your qualification and experiences, and provides references through which these can be checked. In practice, as we have seen, the interviewer confuses this objective information by his subjective judgement at the interview. He allows the dangerous program of liking equals social skills, conscientiousness and reliability, to take over. He has handed the high ground to you.

SELECTION COMMITTEES

It is sometimes thought that the use of a panel to make the assessment will somehow balance out the subjectivity of individual judgement. Unfortunately, as you increase the number of wise judgements being brought to bear, so you increase the number of prejudices and irrelevant factors. Moreover, committees are given to arriving at consensus without thereby improving the quality of their decisions.

You should follow the same basic methods as required for the single interviewer, but remember that you need to form a mini relationship of liking with each committee member. Good eye contact and careful listening to questions will be important. If you can, spot the key person on the committee (they usually speak first and direct the proceedings), you may want to focus a little more often in that direction; but don't forget the others – you will need their helpful influence.

Should you hear that you are about to appear in front of a selection committee, rejoice. The task may be a little more challenging but the outcome is more likely to be in your favour.

STRATEGIES FOR GETTING THAT JOB

- An interviewer will choose you because they like you; but they will think they are choosing you for objective reasons. Your master strategy will be to meet both these needs.
- Apply for many jobs at the same time; you can't have enough offers to enable you to make comparisons and to put you in control. After all, how many candidates are *they* interviewing?
- Compose your application form (or CV) to show why you are qualified and to ensure you get the interview questions you want. Your application must stand out; you can use the

covering letter for this or an introduction from a contact.
pay attention to:
— brevity and simplicity;
— the fact that you should be neither over- nor
  underqualified for the job;
— good written presentation.
- Prepare carefully for the interview; consider how to answer
  the questions so as to appear:
  — reliable and conscientious;
  — independent minded yet similar to the interviewer;
  — to ask questions which the interviewer is proud to
    answer.
- The first impressions program rules so:
  — dress like a successful member of the organisation;
  — flatter by having taken trouble with your appearance;
  — watch your NVC and plan your first answers with
    particular care.
- Once you have an offer you can rely on their commitment to
  find out at last what the job is really about. List your
  questions, negotiate salary, talk to other employees. Then
  decide.

7

Persuasion in business

WHETHER YOU have just started a new job, with the help of Chapter 6, or are wondering how to progress your career with your current employer, you will need to know how to play the persuasion game to advance your career. Why do some people climb the ladder higher and more quickly than their colleagues? You will discover how to do this. How good are you at getting your boss to take up your brilliant ideas? You can learn how to persuade the boss. And, as you move up the ladder, you will want to master the aspects of leadership which make your own team the most effective in the company.

AFTER MANY YEARS as a salesman I moved into my head office with a sense of relief. Although I had greatly enjoyed the process of making sales I was looking forward to a new kind of life in which matters would be settled, not by persuasion, but by a process of rational decisions and instructions being communicated through different levels of the hierarchy.

I was naïve. I quickly discovered that both rational decisions and instructions are rare. The programs which I had learnt to recognise as a salesman seemed to play just as large a part in the responses of my peers and seniors, and instructions turned out to be largely ineffective unless the recipient was induced to accept them with emotional commitment.

There was a difference, of course. In the sales field everyone understands that the salesperson is out to convince and the customer is out to resist. The persuasion game is acknowledged. Within a head office, however, the game lies under the surface. Nevertheless it is at the heart of everything that happens.

Most – perhaps all – of the points about persuasion I have made so far play their part in business. The programs that we have inherited or developed through experience are general; we apply them – with appropriate adaptations – to all the circumstances we encounter, whether these occur in our private or our business lives. But it will be valuable to explore how they affect some functions which are central to business life.

CORPORATE PROGRAMS

Businesses have programs just as individuals do. The persuader who wants to have his or her ideas accepted or get to the top of a company needs to understand what these are and to make use of them – just as he or she must in the conventional persuasion game.

Sol Hershstein became president of a large financial company in Boston, USA. With a hundred years behind it the company was very large, very secure and very slow moving – one of those companies often known as 'sleeping giants'. Sol believed that the future was different and he set about waking the company up. Money was spent on modernisation, new ideas were tried, executives were imported from more vigorous institutions and publicity campaigns were started. The board of directors grew more and more uneasy. Eventually they found an excuse to get rid of Sol and his new imports, and the company went back to sleep.

That was 15 years ago. In the intervening period the future Sol saw came to pass. Eventually the company

> *woke up just before it died in its sleep and Sol's ideas are*
> *working fine. He had chosen the right time to introduce*
> *his ideas from a market point of view, but the wrong*
> *time in terms of company culture.*

The lesson which Sol's experience has for the ambitious executive is to understand the company culture and work with it, rather than against it. Your ideas may be brilliant and put into action they may double profits in the next few years. But, if your ideas run counter to the company's programs, you will achieve no greater success than you will in flouting the programs of an individual. They may be turned down immediately, but the more usual alternative – death by a thousand cuts – is more painful and just as effective. The company's hidden agenda, sometimes known as 'the way we do things here', is its true motivation. Let's look at some examples of corporate programs.

- 'In this company you have to be a financial person in order to get to the top; marketing people are rather vulgar.'
- 'This company does good by stealth. Never talk to the media – if your head's over the parapet you get shot at.'
- 'This company puts all the effort and all the glory into obtaining new business; existing accounts rank second.'
- 'In this company the key people advance themselves by social contacts inside and outside the company. "Who you know" is worth more than "what you know". The galley slaves do the work.'
- 'This company lives by the dictum of Gaius Petronius Arbiter: If you want to give the illusion of progress, reorganise.'
- 'Don't make any mistakes in this company. Providing you initiate nothing but keep your nose clean you will eventually rise to the top.'
- 'This company values new ideas even if they don't always work. Keep them coming or you'll get stuck where you are.'

It is an invaluable exercise to analyse and list in order of influence the programs which operate in the company for which you work. Your analysis should be based on your observation of what happens, rather than any values which the company may claim it observes. To rephrase J. Pierpont Morgan, 'A company generally has two reasons for doing a thing; one that sounds good and a *real* one.' Your analysis will provide you with a ready guide, first enabling you to decide whether this is really the organisation in which you want to make a long-term career and then to give you the programs you will have to use in order to sell your ideas or get to the top.

Getting to the boardroom

Your analysis will include an examination of what sort of people get to the top in your business. For instance, the company may habitually promote from inside or headhunt senior executives from other organisations. If the company is geographically spread, have they promoted people from the centre or taken them from the far-flung reaches? They may be people from the right schools and universities, or more democratic. They may be predominantly financial people, or ideas people, or marketing people.

What do they look like? What do they sound like? Is there a company image to which most of the top people conform?

It could be that you will be the one to change the mould, but – if you want to follow the odds – remember that people tend to like those whom they recognise as similar and tend to trust the people they like.

When you finally make it to the top you will have the opportunity to promote the people *you* like. But be wiser than Sol Hershstein and remember that corporate programs run through the company from top to bottom. Even at the top level it may be better to be seen to be working with the programs, although you may be doing so only to change them. Sol may have had the last laugh, but he is doing it in the outer wilderness of early retirement.

LIGHTNING REMINDER

★ *A company has programs just like an individual; play to them.*

★ *Analyse your company's programs.*

★ *What kind of people get to the top? Be like them.*

SELLING YOUR BOSS

Being a natural persuader we can assume that you are working in a company which is, at least to some degree, open to new ideas. We can also assume that you are confident that the ideas you have will be truly effective. However, this confidence is personal to you; your boss is not yet ready to move over so that you can take his or her seat. How are you going to sell your ideas so that they get accepted and implemented?

The hidden agenda of your boss

Your boss is, of course, keen to advance you; he encourages ideas; he wants to see you make your name. And he will tell you this if you ask him. But before you rely on his declaration of intent you would do well to explore whether your boss, like the rest of the human race, has a hidden agenda, supported by his programs.

● You are likely to find that your boss is closely identified with the corporate programs; after all he is a product of them. He may not have started that way, but his need for consistency and the process of psychological accounting (see Chapter 2) has done its work; he has found it more comfortable to believe in the programs than to reject them. Even if he retains some elements of independcence he knows that, at the practical level, ideas have to conform if they are to be accepted.

- What are your boss's personal ambitions? How are your ideas going to help the boss further up his own ladder?
- What are your boss's values? Does he believe in customer care? Does he believe in the bottom line? Do his views change from time to time, perhaps according to the prominence program (Chapter 1). If so, what is influencing your boss today?
- Does your boss rely on his own opinions or on the advice of others? If the latter, who are the others? What are *their* programs? Is a little preparatory lobbying in order?
- Is your boss susceptible to the herd instinct? Perhaps he is influenced by what other companies are doing; if so, how can you inject the thought that rejecting your idea may leave him out on a limb?
- Your boss may not be prepared to be committed too far; if so, present your idea as a limited experiment – which can quickly be axed. Refrain from discussing the time limit of this experiment or the criteria which will decide its success. Many companies are deriving large profits from ventures which have never formally ceased to be experiments – and have done for decades.
- How does your boss like ideas to be presented? Some like a face-to-face approach, while others like a carefully prepared paper they can read first. Indulge your boss.

Who had the idea?

Remember that the better the idea the greater the threat it contains. Who wants a subordinate who keeps on having better ideas than you do? You will often have to choose between taking credit for an idea and seeing it stifled, or transferring the ownership of the idea to your boss, so that he or she can take the credit. Here are some ways of transferring the ownership of ideas.

- Link them to some earlier, and preferably public, pronouncement of your boss. For instance if the flavour of the month is cost control, point out that the idea is no more

than an extension of his own thinking, and of course
inspired by him.

- Make sure that there is some element in your idea which
your boss will want to change – while leaving the idea
intact. Once the boss's brilliant mind has added the master
touch he will, at least in part, own the idea.

---

*An audio-visual company prepared presentations for
businesses. They always included a picture of the Eiffel
Tower. Their clients would reject the Eiffel Tower and
then accept the presentation wholeheartedly; it had
become their presentation. The company reckoned that
this picture was the most valuable part of their
equipment.*

- Find other ways to confirm your boss's commitment. Ask
him to help you with aspects of the idea you feel need his
experienced attention. Ask him questions and incorporate
the answers. Get him to defend the idea publicly – it
commits him.
- If you know your boss well enough, try the challenge. For
instance, 'I haven't put in any budget allowance for
advertising, because I know how you're determined to keep
that kind of expenditure down.' You may find your boss
telling you, with kindly hand on your shoulder, that he is not
against advertising, only discriminating in his use of it. And
in this case . . .

GETTING A RISE

Let's follow through a practical example in which a fictional
character, Richard Boyle, a computer programmer, sets about
persuading his boss, June Stanton, to increase his salary. This

will enable us to see how an individual might mount a strategy making use of some of the techniques we have already studied. In real life, of course, the process is likely to be neither so orderly nor so thorough.

The motivation triangle

Richard looks first at the Motivation Triangle (Chapter 2). What **Purpose** might June have in handing over more money? He concludes that she will want to retain him because there is a shortage of programmers familiar with the computer language which will be used for a number of important projects that are scheduled. Richard would then be invoking the fear of loss program. This leads to a high risk strategy, because if he fails – and doesn't leave – his credibility will be blown.

Price may be a problem – June has no wish to raise the going rate for programmers and Richard's new level may set a precedent. On the other hand the cost of finding a replacement plus the hidden costs of delaying the work will far outweigh the salary increase.

Probability in this instance is a matter of June being helped to believe that Richard will stay to see the projects through once he has his rise; and will not be tempted to ask again – at least for a reasonable period.

Personal programs

Richard must bear in mind that June is under pressure from the board to reduce costs as far as possible. He also knows that June doesn't like feeling forced to take action – her reactance (see page 173) is strong.

Standard programs

Bearing a well-thumbed copy of this book and checking the Compendium of Programs by referring to Chapter 12, Richard lists ideas that may be helpful to him. These are the ones he selects – although your list might have been different.

- Since he has identified **fear of loss** as important here he must major on this. Can he spring a rumour, using his network, that he is looking elsewhere? He probably knows someone who can be relied upon to inform June without being asked. If she is in the habit of consulting, say, her second in command, he will discuss the whole question – confidentially of course – with that person. He can, of course, put his points much more forcefully to a third party without raising reactance. At the very least he will leave copies of computer appointment advertisements on his desk. He'll need these anyhow for the comparison program.
- **Comparison** will probably be important. Some research that shows he is paid less than the going rate for his job will be an important card and so will any examples of the salary of equivalent jobs in his own organisation. Here the **consistency** program could be fruitful; why should June pay him less than his peers?
- What can he do about June's **frame of reference**? If June is seeing him as just another employee after more money his position will be weak. But if June can be led to see him as an investment in cost-saving technology it will address her personal concern about this – and help her to rationalise (psychological accounting), granting the rise.
- **Reciprocation** may help. If Richard can do June a favour that is not obviously connected to his request, that will help. Or perhaps he might volunteer to take a trainee programmer under his wing – with the additional security that will reassure her there will be continuity on these important projects.

Moods are contagious. If you want your boss to be enthusiastic, you'd better be enthusiastic yourself. If you want them to be concerned about profits, this is the feeling you must transmit. Bad moods are contagious, too. If your request for a rise sounds like a moan it will cause a similar moan to rise in your boss's breast.

Richard's strategy

With these ideas in mind Richard plans his strategy; in doing
so, further programs suggest themselves.

He decides that he will follow the high risk strategy of fear of
loss since he does not believe that any other purpose will be
strong enough to move June. He briefly considers, but
dismisses in this case, ways of making June believe that she
thought of the idea first. However she has occasionally used the
phrase, 'If you pay peanuts you get monkeys.' So he may have
a chance to refer to that, at least obliquely.

To help raise his value, and therefore the extent of the loss,
he capitalises on some recent work he has been doing which
demonstrates how well the projects are going and confirms
their value to the company. He times this so that the report will
be with June shortly before his interview. In this way he will
employ the prominence program and also the first impressions
program. Indeed, he might start the interview by briefly
discussing the report to ensure that she is in a good mood. This
could be an opportunity to suggest how keen he is to coach a
trainee programmer; this would show his enthusiasm to see the
projects through – while opening up the desirability of
reciprocation. He will, of course, be using good non verbal
communication himself – and judging carefully from June's
NVC the best moment at which to steer the conversation down
the course he has in mind.

While he hopes the rumour that he is looking elsewhere will
have reached June, he is going to have to tackle this directly.
Knowing her susceptibility to reactance he will need to be
careful. In the end he decides on some phrasing like this:

*I need to talk to you about money, June. Perhaps you
could advise me. I see from the appointment columns –
and also my friends in the industry tell me – that my sort
of job is usually paid about 20 per cent more in the
leading companies than I get here. Now you know that
I'm as keen as mustard about getting these projects
completed – not least because they mean so much for*

cost control in the company, but I wonder whether I don't owe it to my family to get closer to the going rate. You see my dilemma? What do you think?

That innocent speech addresses purpose, price and probability – while dampening down any reactance. June is being asked for her advice, not receiving a demand. Besides, if it were Richard alone he wouldn't have raised the subject – but it's his family; and who can blame someone for fulfilling his duty? Into that speech he has worked one of June's values (cost control) and appealed to the herd instinct (what other leading companies pay). June may not notice these directly, but they will have their effect.

Mark Twain tells of the occasion when a preacher was making an appeal for funds. After his opening paragraphs Twain was ready to give a generous sum. But as the address went on and on, the amount he was prepared to give became less and less.

So keep your initial presentation simple and don't try to prove too much. There will be plenty of opportunity to bring in further points later on – but only if they are needed.

Richard will wait to see how June reacts to this; and he will use good listening (see Chapter 10) before responding. But he will certainly have thought through the possible defences she may use and considered how he will deal with them. Here are some defences she might try.

- June may try a delaying tactic. After all it's quite reasonable for her to want to think the matter over. But Richard has his diary with him and suggests a date when they could talk further about it. Notice that he is not demanding an answer – only to talk further. Perhaps she will consult the second in command Richard has already spoken to. And that next meeting will undoubtedly decide the matter.

- She may be sceptical about the ease with which Richard can get 20 per cent more elsewhere. While not giving the impression that he has prepared too carefully to shoot her down, he will casually mention the evidence he has gleaned.
- She may try bargaining. But Richard is ready for that. He has planted the 20 per cent figure so that the lower figure he is willing to accept eventually will seem cheap to June, and also something of a concession on his part. (See bargaining in Chapter 8.) That way June will *feel* she's won; Richard will *know* that he has.

We could continue following through Richard's contingency planning, but the picture so far is enough to demonstrate how a skilled player might set about the task in a clear-cut persuasion situation.

STRATEGIES FOR PERSUADING YOUR BOSS

- Analyse the task in terms of Purpose, Price and Probability. How are you going to satisfy each of these?
- Review your boss's agendas; he is more likely to accept an idea that benefits him, than one which benefits you. What are the boss's values? His ambitions? On whose opinions does the boss rely?
- Think of ways in which you can give your boss ownership of the idea.
  - Can you link to an idea the boss has already expressed?
  - Can you leave the boss room to modify the idea and therefore assume ownership?
  - Can you use the boss's reactance to challenge him to champion the idea?
- Using your general knowledge of programs, pick the ones that will help. Avoid programs which may hinder.
- Check that your mood is right. Be enthusiastic about your

idea, but don't rush at your boss. Remember, he needs to feel he's helping you. Keep much of your ammunition in reserve – you may not need it and it will have more impact when used to answer his questions or difficulties.

PERSUADING YOUR STAFF

Persuading staff involves the new dimension of maintaining effective persuasion throughout long-term relationships. Some adaptation of the methods we have discussed so far will be needed, but the basic principles remain much the same.

The law of first impressions

> *At one stage in my brief military career I was temporarily in charge of a transport company. When the real commanding officer arrived I was amazed at the brusque energy with which he set about restoring the efficiency which he deemed my amateurishness had allowed to deteriorate. After three weeks of this he changed modes and, as far as I could see, did absolutely nothing for the next several months. But the law of first impressions had worked and no one in the company doubted that he was a tough egg who had everything under iron control.*

You may have the opportunity from time to time, as I have had, to benefit from that lesson. You set your stamp of authority and the standards you want to inculcate from the very first day. Instead of following your instinct to ingratiate yourself with a new staff to wean them from loyalty to any predecessor you do just the opposite. Within a short space of time you have extinguished past habits and set new ones. And the new ones will persist.

This is harder to do if you have been promoted from within the group – remember that the prophet has no honour in his own country. You may be helped by taking a long holiday prior to your appointment or – even better – a management course. But your new staff should know within hours of your move into your new office that you are a completely different person. They will curse you, they will accuse you of disloyalty, they will try to hurt you. And you will be hurt. But if you can hold the line you will establish a new and acceptable leadership personality in a matter of days. Compromise and it may take you months – if you succeed at all.

The stamp of authority

I do not advocate following this military lesson to its ultimate, which would mean relying on the effects of first impressions indefinitely. You will need from time to time to re-exert your authority through tough actions. In between, your good manners, your charm and your consideration will be all the more valued by contrast. Senior members of the royal family are often praised for their graciousness. What would be seen as simple courtesy and consideration in others is reputed to be high virtue in an authority figure.

Resist the temptation to become 'one of the gang'. Your authority should be backed up by a subtle element of separation. Of course you join in the social occasions but as a visitor rather than as a participant. While having a general affection for members of your staff, you avoid any special friendships; these not only damage your friends but make it difficult to maintain your reputation for fairness and objectivity. Leadership and loneliness go together.

You might think that a degree of authoritarian remoteness will make it difficult for you to inspire your staff. But that is to forget the strong obedience program described in Chapter 3. While your subordinates may occasionally resent your authority and will undoubtedly be slanderous behind your back, they actually *need* it. How can they feel safe when their leader is obviously of common clay like them? How can a boss inspire them when the boss holds no greater height than they? Indulge their need. The leader who sinks to the common level may have short-term popularity, but it will be followed by long-term disaster. The leader who, despite his or her openness and informality, still retains the charisma of authority will get the best of both worlds.

Leadership style

The obedience program, powerful as it is, is not absolute. While the pre-human hunting band knew that it was necessary to tolerate some failure on the leader's part, because continuous changes of leadership are inefficient, the point can come when faith is lost. Successful leaders can be forgiven much, but the leader who cannot bring home the metaphorical bacon will either be toppled or ignored.

This makes the success of the group the pre-eminent objective. In some contexts that means a leadership style which gives subordinates responsibility and freedom of action; in others it means a strict regime in which adherence to defined and detailed standards keeps the operation cost-effective, so preserving jobs and wages. There is no such thing as one ideal leadership style. But, broadly speaking, the evidence suggests that the more complex and creative the task, the more the leadership style should incline towards building personal responsibility in the team members. As technology reduces repetitive tasks and increases the importance of knowledge workers, this style needs to become more common. But in the end your ideal leadership style is the one which best blends the character of the task with your own natural ways of behaving. That is the one that is most likely to work.

The world outside

Shrewd observers of human nature, from Socrates to Machiavelli, have described what every leader should know: outside enemies bind the group. This characteristic must have been bred in the very earliest times when our ancestors learnt a program which said: the more the danger the more we must rely on everyone playing their part in support of the group. Whether one is talking about adolescent gangs, or countries, or groups within business the threat from outside creates unity inside. It is not healthy for different sections of a business to be at loggerheads with one another, but a leader should certainly tolerate, or even implicitly encourage, a degree of rivalry with the forces outside. The leader's particular group is of higher quality, works more effectively, has more style than the others. They are not enemies, we co-operate with them of course, but *we* are something of an élite.

The good leader includes an ambassadorial role. This goes both ways. His wider knowledge of company affairs gives him authority to communicate senior management's wishes to the group; it also enables him to represent the group to senior management. Do the bosses know just how good the group is? Is the leader fiercely loyal to the group where outsiders are concerned – irrespective of how he treats the group inside? Do the leader's people have a better chance of promotion because of his skilled advocacy of the group's interests? Do they get the right facilities and equipment to do their job? Is the work of the group influential in the company's plans?

Who cares, wins

We looked at the reciprocation program in Chapter 1 and saw the power of the deep instinct to reciprocate gifts. In this context the gift is the active concern of the leader that each individual should succeed in his task and move towards achieving his personal objectives. Staff are bound by the program to repay this care by loyalty and determination to live up to what is expected of them.

It may be possible to simulate such personal concern but, because it has to be demonstrated by deeds rather than words – and over a long period of time – this is difficult. Fortunately this does not require liking – it is unreasonable to expect that a leader will like every member of his staff equally, just as parents may find they do not like all their children equally, but are nevertheless bound to show them equal concern.

> *A study was carried out some years ago to discover whether salespeople in successful and unsuccessful teams viewed their managers differently. Not surprisingly they did. But the major differences were not in their perception of their manager's professional skills or the manager's personality. The factors which counted, besides enthusiasm for the task itself, were unselfishness, co-operation and interest in the salespeople's success.*

LIPS

All this brings us back to the limited image performance syndrome again (see page 53). As we have seen, the effective leader is concerned with the self-image of the group. If they see themselves as an élite, that is how they will behave. Since the focus of achievement is on the success of the group this is how they will interpret what éliteness means for them.

In showing concern for each individual the leader will work very hard to raise their personal LIPS. In order to do this the leader must understand the personal motivations and programs of his people, and discover ways in which achieving these will contribute to the task. He will always look for the potential strengths which can be developed rather than the weaknesses to be eradicated. His strategy is to raise those strengths to a level where the weaknesses are a small price to pay or where the strengths themselves eradicate the weaknesses.

> *An interesting study of appraisal interviews showed that, following the interview, the staff member built on the good points that had been identified by the boss but did little to improve the weak points. However, when necessary, weak points can be tackled by agreeing definite, timed and monitored objectives for correction. In this way, each milestone of improvement becomes*

> *itself a positive achievement; and the ability to correct faults becomes part of the good self-image.*

Robert Townsend recalls how he was told, when he first took over the Avis company, that he would need a whole new top team. Three years later the same people were so changed that the problem was not finding a successor for Townsend, but choosing between too many suitable candidates. That's how good leadership works.

> *There are dangers in good leadership of course. One friend of mind began to get irritated when colleagues discounted his efforts by pointing out how lucky he was to have first-class subordinates. Eventually he felt obliged to exclaim that throughout his management career he always seemd to be lucky with his subordinates – wasn't that an odd coincidence?*
>
> *But even he had missed one factor. His style of leadership gave his people such a strong sense of fulfilment that all the best people in the company tried to join him whenever he had a vacancy.*

The big organisation

Applying these principles to the larger organisation does not alter them. But it does mean that you have to work through your second line management. That's good because, like Townsend, you will be preparing your subordinates for bigger jobs.

> *If you have a subordinate who wants to get a bigger job outside the organisation, and you cannot genuinely foresee their ambition being satisfied reasonably soon within the organisation, help them to get it. Not only will you free up the promotion ladder for someone else,*

> *but you will have demonstrated that none of your people will suffer by growing too tall. In fact, good leaders usually have the opposite problem – no one wants to leave them. And that can cause a log jam.*

Teach your subordinates to handle their own people as you handle them. Your major method will be through example. But you will also be working on their self-images as managers and leaders. You will be modifying their behaviour by indicating in a thousand ways your approval for activities which are along the right lines.

It is a myth to think that the chiefs of large organisations usually work through careful master plans which document in detail the objectives and the strategies to follow. They do, of course, have a compelling idea of where the organisation is going and they have their own general principles which they believe are necessary to get it there. But in successful organisations they tend to communicate all of this, not by barking orders, but by a process of continuous shaping. They give examples, they ask questions, they respond appropriately to information they receive from all quarters, and they reinforce through verbal and non verbal approval actions which support the objectives.

It works because of the authority and obedience patterns we have studied. All eyes are on the leader with authority. We are programmed to look to the leader for how we behave, how we think, even how we feel. We do this willingly and unconsciously because aeons ago our ancestors learnt that this was the way to survive.

STRATEGIES FOR PERSUASIVE LEADERSHIP

- Establish yourself as a leader early. You are no longer 'one of the gang'.

- Base your leadership style on the nature of the task to be done. But prefer to delegate initiative and responsibility when this is possible.
- Give your group identity by promoting rivalry with other groups, but maintaining the necessary co-operation.
- Be the effective ambassador, representing and defending your group with loyalty.
- Genuine care for your group is essential; they will reciprocate.
- Work continually to raise the self-image of the group and its individual members.
- If your organisation is large teach your subordinates to imitate your methods. Give them room to move – so work at shaping the organisation rather than listing detailed orders. The obedience program is on your side.

Persuasion in the outside world

8

Fair exchange: selling and negotiation

THE PROFESSIONAL persuasion game is played by those who sell and negotiate for a living. The skills, the programs and the strategies we have been learning about are used to the full. But you don't need to be a salesperson to benefit. In fact we are all sales people and negotiators in our private lives. Here we look at how the professional game is played, and we learn both how to play the cards that separate the professional from the amateur and, equally important, how to defend ourselves against them.

SELLING AND NEGOTIATION are the natural playing fields of the persuasion game. Psychologists, undertaking studies of how people are persuaded, have often started by observing salespeople in action. They rightly supposed that the tricks of that trade would only have been developed if they had proved effective.

HOW MUCH DO YOU KNOW ABOUT SALES TACTICS?

Here's a quiz to find out. Check your answers against the information in this chapter.

1. You are not sure whether you want the product. The salesperson explains to you that it is in short supply and this may be your last chance. Does this make it

    More desirable? Less desirable? Makes no difference?

2. You have told the salesman that you only have £10,000 available for a new car; but he shows you one at £14,000, first. Will this

    Simply annoy you? Raise your sights? Make no difference?

3. You are considering taking out a life assurance policy. The salesperson mentions that she sold a policy to a well-known pop singer last week. Do you think:

    What do pop singers know about it? I don't believe her? It must be a good policy then?

4. There is a tempting display of green vegetables in your supermarket. Is this because:

    They are very fresh? Beautifully arranged? They are bathed in green electric light?

5. A telephone salesperson is talking about a product you don't want; you can't seem to get rid of him. Do you:

    Explain why you're not interested? Put the phone down while the salesperson is talking? Put the phone down while you're talking?

EVERYONE A SALESMAN?

A great deal of all our lives is spent in some form of selling and negotiation. Let's take an imaginary couple – John and Mary Blunt – and look at some of the transactions they handle in an ordinary day.

> *It starts with the alarm clock. Who makes the tea? That's a negotiation. Who gets the car and who goes to work by bus? Then there's some negotiation at breakfast because their son wants to play computer games with a friend after school, and John and Mary want to make sure he finishes his school project.*
>
> *At work John has to negotiate some service contracts with a supplier, and he's also got to talk another manager into lending him an extra member of staff for a week. There's a price to pay for that, you can be sure. Mary is going to ask her boss for a rise; she thinks she'll get it because she's willing to take on more responsibility. But she'll leave it until the afternoon because she has hopes of signing up a new customer for a substantial stationery order in the morning. That will lend force to her case.*
>
> *John has undertaken to go to the vegetable market during his lunch hour, but Mary won't have time for shopping. However, she's going to look in at the furniture showroom on her way home because they've promised themselves a new suite this year.*

Each of those transactions involves a price or an exchange. We recognise the obvious ones such as John's vegetables or Mary's stationery order. But what bargain will they make with their son over homework? What will Mary have to do to get her rise? You might care to cast your mind back over the past day or two and see just how many sales or negotiations you have taken part in – even though you may not have thought of them as such.

SOME BASIC PRINCIPLES

The essence of a sale is contained in the three points of the Motivation Triangle: Purpose, Price and Probability. The salesperson must address **Purpose** through establishing the customer's wants; demonstrate how their product will meet those wants (**Probability**); present **Price** so that it seems worth paying to achieve the Purpose. Negotiation follows the same pattern, except that both people are paying a Price and both must, on balance, be satisfied on the other points.

Understanding needs and wants

Dale Carnegie, in *How to Win Friends and Influence People*, argued that the first principle is to find out what a person wants and help them to get it. This truth, which permeates this book, emphasises that the foundation on which good bargains are made is the knowledge of the needs and wants of the other party.

The salesperson-negotiator must be aware of the want which triggers buying action; it may not be immediately obvious:

> *Early man cannot be described as having wanted the wheel. They were obliged to move heavy objects around and presumably they dragged them in some kind of sledge or, later, by using tree trunks as rollers. When someone showed them how to make a permanent roller by using an axle, they still didn't want a wheel as such. What they wanted was convenience and efficiency, and the roller with axle satisfied their want.*
>
> *Similarly, people don't want television sets, they want in-house entertainment; they don't want cars, they want transport and prestige.*

Needs and wants are not necessarily the same. I may need to lose weight but I may not want to. I may want a car which does

150 m.p.h., but I may not need one. The distinction is important because people act on wants rather than needs and until the salesperson-negotiator can transform a need into a want they will not get the action they seek. Needs are in the head, wants are in the heart.

Benefits versus features

The salesperson therefore talks in terms of benefits rather than features. Few customers, for instance, are tempted by the presence of a technological feature in, say, a television for its own sake, but they will be interested if it gives them a better picture. They may discover that they have wants they never suspected – such as a stereo sound system – once they have had its potential advantages explained.

> *In some cases the feature itself is the benefit. For instance customers may be tempted by a sound system which has features from which they will never benefit because they have cloth ears and an unsubtle taste in music. But the presence of the feature makes them feel good and they can mention it to their friends.*

Reactance

Reactance is the name of the program which makes us resent, often with irrational levels of emotion, having our backs pressed up against the wall. A struggle of wills is involved. Skilled salespeople-negotiators try to avoid this by suggesting that their positions are dictated by outside factors. Thus a buyer of factory equipment may fight the price, not because they won't pay it, but because, they claim they cannot make a profit with it on those terms. Negotiators often deal through agents because it keeps the level of emotion down, and the difficulties can be laid at the principal's door, rather than the negotiator's. Sometimes a principal (or a principal's view) is invented – 'I don't disagree with your terms; unfortunately I can't persuade my partner (wife, boss) to agree.'

Salespeople-negotiators often use phrases like 'It's entirely up to you' or 'Only you can judge whether that's right'. And they ask questions which enable them to present their offering as a response to their opponent's expressed needs. They know that, once reactance sets in, bargaining will be replaced by obstinacy.

> *The print unions in Britain were in a powerful position since few newspapers could withstand a prolonged strike. As a result over-manning and restrictive practices were widespread, and new technology was resisted. Eventually, newspaper proprietors took dramatic action and built new works with modern machinery that were not dependent on the unions. The print unions lost because they failed to compromise between their needs and those of the proprietors.*

The best bargains are made when both parties, while seeking advantage for themselves, look to the wants of the other. Not only is the bargain likely to be concluded, but its terms are also likely to stick and reactance is not provoked.

Fear of loss

This basic program applies widely in sales and negotiations. A benefit becomes more desirable when we may not be able to get it and less desirable if it is readily available. The appeal of the limited bargain or the temporary cut-price sale is made in every high street. Do you ever get the impression that some business houses are perpetually in the process of closing down?

In the face-to-face sale the same tactic is often used – perhaps this is the last model in the shop or a special concession needs to be made in order to meet your needs. Of course this can go both ways. Just as the seller can pretend that the customer is lucky to have the opportunity to buy, so the customer can become a rare commodity by not being altogether sure whether they want to buy, or making it clear that they have plenty of opportunities to buy elsewhere.

> *Cialdini, in* Influence, Science and Practice, *tells how his brother paid for his college fees by selling second-hand cars. He would arrange for all enquirers to call at the same time. The first enquirer would be quite offhand, until the second enquirer arrived and was asked to wait a few minutes. If that didn't force the sale, the arrival of the third enquirer undoubtedly would.*

Reciprocation

The essence of bargaining is reciprocation. That is, when we offer a concession on price or terms, we call this program into action to induce the other party to match our 'gift'. We can readily see how this happens in an orthodox negotiation, but it can also happen in a sale where the price tag is apparently fixed. The salesperson, for example, can give a better trade-in price, or offer freebies – 'I'll put in a pack of free video tapes for you'. The customer can play the same game – 'I'll take this shop-soiled model, if you give me the right price on it'. Or, 'If I take those headphones as well, what price will you charge for the two together?'

The final concession can be effectively reserved until the last moment. Just as the customer is using her comparison program for her final decision, the salesperson throws in one extra benefit or reduction to tip the scales.

Selling from the top down

Closely related to reciprocation is the common technique of raising the customer's sights. Here the salesperson starts by offering models which are above the customer's stated price range – and then moving down the scale. The result is that the customer buys towards the top of their price range; the opposite tactic – usually the sign of the amateur salesperson – is to start at the bottom, hoping that cheapness will make the sale. The customer is then likely to buy at the bottom of his price range.

Low ball procedure

A different approach is to settle for a straightforward sale and then to suggest extras which will enhance the basic purchase. Each addition is seen as only a small extra cost, through the comparison program – and we think of them one by one, rather than looking at the total we have bought. It can happen that a customer who believes they have, with due economy, settled for the basic model of a car, ends up with all the features, and the price, of the luxury model – except for the badge.

ADVANCED SELLING

The programs I have described so far are both basic and important for any successful selling. When we turn to the sale of intangibles, like a financial service, some additional factors must be taken into account.

The personality sale

Because the product is intangible – it cannot be seen or felt or properly tested – much more depends on the way in which the salesperson projects his or her personality. If the customer does not trust either the salesperson's knowledge or their honesty, no sale will take place. Much of their energy must therefore be devoted to this.

Establishing the wants

If we walk into a television shop or a car salesroom, it is a reasonable inference that we have at least some desire to make a purchase – although the salesperson will start by trying to establish our wants in more detail. But in a life assurance sale, for instance, it is quite likely that the customer is not aware that they have any want or need for the product. Consequently a feature of the sales process will be to establish this in some detail.

Let's look at some of the programs which can play a part in the sale of intangibles.

Programs for the advanced sale

- First impressions – manner, clothes, speaking voice – will be key. The salesperson will, in most instances, only be in contact with the customer for an hour or two before the decision is made; unless the salesperson can convey that he is honest, knowledgeable and low pressure within the first few minutes, he might as well stop there.

> *One leading company taught its salespeople to 'smile as you dial'. They believed that the smile (a program we met in Chapter 4) came across in the voice and in the relaxed manner of the conversation.*
>
> *Frank Bettger a great life assurance salesman, tells how he deliberately smiled to himself before calling on a new customer. The smile was still traced on his lips as he gave his greeting.*

- Endorsement by a third party, perhaps a former customer or a mutual friend, can play an important part in first impressions. Endorsement is a program which, while sharing in herd instinct, works most directly through the power of association. If someone you respect endorses a product or a person, some of that respect is transferred to the product itself. It is not always necessary for the endorser to be in any way a qualified judge – as may be seen from advertisements in which attractive showbusiness figures are seen endorsing products about which they have no apparent expertise. The association with attraction, and the credibility it engenders, may be enough.

- The salesperson must be skilled in asking the questions which lead the customer to reveal his own need. For example, questions along the lines of, 'What would be the minimum income which Mary and the children would need in the event of your death?' followed by, 'Tell me how much income will be provided in the event of your death on the basis of your current arrangements,' will allow the customer to discover the gap for himself. This is an instance of the ownership program, which we saw in the last chapter. The principle is simple: we are more motivated by the ideas we have reached ourselves than those we are simply told about.

  Another program involved here is consistency; when we have discovered the need for ourselves, and admitted it, it is inconsistent not to take remedial action.

- The salesperson will try to phrase questions so that the answer will usually be 'yes', thus building a series of positive agreements. He will give little summaries of the decisions so far, making it difficult for the customer to retreat without feeling inconsistent.

- The salesperson will usually have some diagrams or illustrations which require him to sit beside the customer, thus avoiding sitting opposite in a confrontational mode (see Chapter 4).

- The salesperson will make references to other customers, thus employing herd instinct. For example, 'The level of contribution I am suggesting is the one which I find most people in your circumstances are able to meet without too much difficulty. But please tell me if it is too much or too little.' Notice that the word 'contribution' is used instead of 'premium' (the language program) and that reactance is avoided by allowing the customer to disagree.

- The salesperson will turn objections into questions: 'You're wondering whether it's right to start this immediately, given that you still have an overdraft to clear. Is that your worry?' This is a confirmation that this is a problem-solving exercise in which the salesperson is assisting the customer, rather than a sale.

- The salesperson builds up customers' LIPS by treating them as if they were the provident, thoughtful and caring people they would really like to be.

- The salesperson will explain, and even emphasise, the disadvantages of the solution – 'I want you to understand that this is a long-term proposition; surrender values in the early years will be less than you've paid in. Have I made that clear?' – so that the salesperson raises his credibility on all the key points.

- The salesperson will use motivational anecdotes at all major points in the interview because of their power to persuade.

- The salesperson will change the customer's frame of reference, particularly when wanting to bring the value of the benefits forward in the customer's mind. 'Imagine that you died yesterday. Today you are your wife, reviewing the future financial picture for you and the children. What is going through your mind?'

- Knowing that delay is the most frequent excuse to avoid buying the salesperson will build anti-delay factors into the presentation. For instance, he may be able to use a prospective change in the tax benefits of a plan to urge immediate purchase. Or he might use fear of loss by showing how delay will lose the customer eventual benefits. He may also use fear of loss by pointing out that the customer has to qualify medically for the plan; it is not just a question of whether the customer will apply for it, but also whether the company will be prepared to accept the customer.

- As he approaches the close of the sale the salesperson will ask 'ownership' questions, such as: 'Would you want your plan to contain waiver of premium benefits?' These will also give the salesperson a clue on how ready the customer is to buy.

- The salesperson will close the sale by asking the customer to choose alternatives. For instance: 'Would you like to make your contributions annually in advance, or would monthly be better?' The customer concentrates on the alternatives and never feels he is making a decision.

- The salesperson will ask the customer to check the application form and read the small print. Thus the salesperson's trustworthiness is made prominent at a crucial moment and the customer is relieved of any sense of pressure which might cause reactance.
- The salesperson will have prepared figures to enable him to negotiate. Thus it is easy for him to demonstrate altered benefits if the customer wants to change the premium.
- The salesperson will reassure a hesitant customer that the customer has an opportunity to change his or her mind before matters are irrevocably concluded. Salespeople know that in almost every instance a combination of commitment and inertia will ensure that the sale sticks.

That is a formidable, if incomplete, list of the programs which the advanced salesperson might use. It may be a relief to realise that, even with this armoury at their disposal, an experienced financial services salesperson will only complete about one sale for every three attempts.

THE NEGOTIATION

Most sales, as we have seen, contain elements of negotiation; that is, both players have some room to vary the terms on which they will do business − and therefore they bargain until they are both happy that their wants are being adequately met. But we most frequently think of negotiation when the players are entirely free to settle their terms and when the exchange taking place involves a number of issues which need to be agreed. The parties do not think of themselves as buyers or sellers, but as two equals who have benefits to exchange.

Strategies for negotiation

- Negotiation is like poker. If you haven't got the better hand, it's all the more important to play it as if you had. But be ready to throw your cards in once you know you're on to a loser.
- Negotiations succeed best if both players are able to meet their wants. So look for ways in which your opponent's wants can be met without unacceptably endangering your own. Know the market you are entering and be realistic about what you can achieve.
- Research your opponent's needs – both rational and psychological. What programs are driving them? Research your own needs – and decide in advance at what level these must be met for you to agree. You may be wise to write down the upper and lower limits you will accept; this will remind you to review the bargain with fresh eyes as the situation changes.
- Research the deal and note all the angles. Any of the items, even minor ones, may be useful as a lever, a bargaining point or a 'gift' requiring reciprocation.
- Get to know your opponent; this is an opportunity not only for research but to get him or her to like and trust you. But remember that both of you can be fooled by this if you don't watch out.
- In certain negotiations you may want to use an agent, to get tough bargaining without reactance. House purchase is a common example. But if one is used against you, remember that agents' effective authority is wider than they would have you believe, that they are susceptible to their own needs and programs, that they can work for your side even if the other side is paying.
- Plan your negotiation carefully. What terms most favourable to you will you start with? What concessions will you make and in what order? What pressures can you bring to bear? Remember that a negotiation should never become a battle of wills involving reactance, so prepare your rationalisations for the terms you need. What will you agree

to initially and what further advantages will you seek at the right psychological moments?

- Everything is negotiable, although it may not always be apparent. You can negotiate for goods, for services, for facilities. You can negotiate with shops and businesses, with friends, with your boss and your staff, with your spouse and with your children. The general principles of negotiation can be adapted to every situation.

THE SUPERMARKET SALE

We might think that buying in a supermarket is a straightforward operation: there are the goods, each marked with a non negotiable price; you are free to pick or reject − and all you have to do is to pay. But it's not that simple. The supermarket managers know a thing or two about selling programs. Here are a few examples.

- Measurement of eye-blink rate indicates that shoppers' brains largely close down when faced by the abundance of goodies on every side. It's a perfect state to enlist automatic programs. The eye-blink rate goes up as the shopper approaches the check-out.
- You may think that you choose your own route when you go around the supermarket. You may not be aware that the placing of the entrance has been chosen to capitalise on our tendency to move clockwise around spaces. Or that goods are arranged so that we are exposed to the maximum temptation before we get to the staple goods everyone has to buy.
- Do you choose the pace at which you move around? Typically, the supermarket will have quite narrow aisles for low margin, staple goods. Customers move down quickly, grabbing from side to side. Higher margin goods are set in the wider aisles. We relax, slow down and give ourselves browsing time to make the more self-indulgent purchases.

The liquor section may even have zig-zag aisles to slow us down some more. And watch out for the Muzak – it's carefully chosen to get us in the right mood and moving at the right pace.

- End-of-aisle displays are very effective. Manufacturers will pay more to get their goods displayed there because they sell so well. There might be a carefully chosen selection of related goods – for barbecuing, for instance; or what looks like a casually filled bin of an impulse product. But there's nothing casual about it.

- Beautifully prepared joints of meat brightly lit in eye-level freezers attract the eye. And how about those wonderfully green vegetables? They are wonderfully green because they're suffused in green light. They may well be placed close to the entrance to tempt you inside.

> *In some large American supermarkets a free coffee machine is installed. How much does it cost them to provide coffee for all those customers? How much extra profit do they make from customers whose shopping exhaustion is relieved by a caffeine break?*

Supermarket design, layout and pricing is based on careful studies of buying behaviour. But you may think that, not being one of the crowd, you are invulnerable to such techniques. Perhaps. But a better strategy may be to accept that you are and then compensate for it. You may have the discipline to make a shopping list beforehand and stick to it no matter what. Or, simply through understanding the techniques, you may be able to raise your awareness, keep your eye-blink rate high and override your brain's automatic responses to the programs the supermarket manager is trying to enlist.

LIGHTNING REMINDER

★ *Supermarkets are professional persuaders; they will use every legitimate card in the pack.*

★ *Take a trip around a supermarket and see how many ploys you can spot. Then at least you'll know what you're up against.*

HOW TO COUNTER THE HARD SELL

You may think that the use of many of the programs described in this chapter comes under the heading of the hard sell. If so, you should now be better equipped to counter-attack. But there is a different kind of hard sell of which we need to be aware. If persuasion programs represent the skilful use of the rapier, the alternative might be described as putting the boot in. Its characteristic is that of the bully − not in terms of physical force but through social embarrassment, manipulating our soft heartedness or our unwillingness to answer a boot with a boot.

One example of this might be the 'student' sale. These are alleged students who come to your door and tell you they are working their way through college and if only you'll buy their goods you'll be helping their grand endeavours. Dare you turn them away and damage such a worthy cause?

Sometimes it is not a student but the representative of a charity. Charities, with the very best of intentions, can find themselves using moral pressures which are very hard to resist.

A young and impoverished couple were flattered at being asked to a smart evening party by an older friend of theirs. Half-way through the evening everyone sat down and the guests were addressed on the subject of a particular charity. Then they were all asked to pledge, out loud, how much they would give. Large sums were volunteered, but the young couple, who were wondering how they were going to meet their mortgage at the end

|| *of the month, had the courage to sit out their* ||
|| *embarrassment and say nothing. Good for them.* ||

Another type of hard sell comes on the telephone where a great variety of goods and services may be offered. The problem is the persistent sales person who will not accept that we choose not to see them. Once again our natural good manners lead us into giving reasons for this; which is then countered by the caller who has heard all the reasons before and knows exactly how to answer them. And, if we yield, we may find the salesperson who visits us to be a very persistent guest – only too happy to outstay his welcome if a sale is in the air.

Start your defence by getting your attitude right. Turn back to the section on *Who has the problem?* in Chapter 3. The salesperson has the job of getting sales and he knows that only a small proportion of attempts will yield results. Accepting rejection is part of what he is paid for. If you reject him firmly, he has the problem. No doubt he can solve it by approaching his next prospective customer – but that's his business. If you don't reject him, or subject yourself to the painful experience of trying to get off the hook, you have volunteered to take the problem on to your shoulders. More fool you.

The hard salesperson starts with the advantage – at least of practice – and very often of training too. We can be trapped by our inability to think up negative reasons as quickly as the professional can produce well-rehearsed positive reasons. So it's wise to prepare yourself with some simple counter-moves.

● If you don't like buying at the door, respond instantly with: 'I'm sorry, we never buy at the door. Thank you for calling.' And close the door firmly and without hesitation. It's so simple, isn't it? (It is wise, particularly if you are alone in the house, to keep the security chain on.) Notice that the good manners you use actually help your case; it makes it sound as if you are acting on principle and we have a program which says 'don't interfere with people's principles'. The 'principle' rejoinder is also useful for requests to take part in lotteries for charitable causes. 'I never take part in lotteries' suggests that one disapproves of such forms of gambling.

- The rattling charity tin should never cause you to divert your path to avoid it. If you don't want to give, look at the collector with a firm smile, even say good morning and pass by. You may or may not have given already; and you don't wear a charity badge because you prefer not to be ostentatious about your virtue.

- Telephone solicitations require a similar treatment to callers at the door. Assuming you're not interested, simply say: 'I'm not interested but thank you for calling' and put the receiver down. Don't give way to your natural instinct to pause for a reply; it's the chink the caller needs. Should you find yourself engaged in dialogue, it's not too late to cut it off. If it goes against the grain to extinguish the caller in mid-flow you can always disconnect while *you* are speaking. This tip is useful for any telephone call you would like to bring to an end without undue offence.

- Put-off responses such as 'I'll think about it' or 'Put your proposition in writing' are, unless they happen to be sincere, unworthy of the games player. When you feel 'no', you say 'no' and leave the problem where it belongs.

This is not intended as an attack on salespeople, charity collectors or suchlike. They contribute much to society through the services they offer. But, just as they are free to contact you, so they must accept your freedom to refuse discussion if you are not interested. It is general experience that the more successful a salesperson, the less he uses hard sell tactics. He does not need and cannot afford to waste his time on someone who is not interested in discussing his product.

LIGHTNING REMINDER

★ *The hard sell works because we allow ourselves to be trapped by social embarrassment, false guilt and soft-heartedness.*

★ *Remember, you decide who has the problem – it will be either your opponent or you.*

★ *Study your counter-moves: hard sell tactics require hard defences.*

9

Persuading the System

THE SYSTEM is out to beat us; so we need to know how to beat the System. Tackling bureaucrats is not hard, indeed almost a pleasure, when you know how to do it. And similar methods can be used for other people who try to balk us. Forming a powerful pressure group is a skill to master; so is the best way to deal with those irritating neighbours. The 'experts' can make formidable opponents, but there are ways of cutting them down to size.

EVERYONE has their anecdotes about the System. Whether it is incompatible regulations, a need to get a complaint dealt with successfully, persuading a receptionist that a doctor should make a house call, getting in to see the one person who can help or a thousand and one other needs – the System presents a blank wall. We sometimes feel that there is a conspiracy of bureaucrats whose purpose in life is to balk us at every turn.

This chapter is about beating the System. Many of the persuasion techniques you have studied in this book will prove helpful, but here I will concentrate on a number of effective strategies which are capable of getting through blank walls and making the System work *for* you rather than against you. None of the strategies is infallible, but you can be sure they will improve the odds.

THE BUREAUCRAT

Bureaucrats are usually to be found at the heart of the System and it is wise to consider how their minds work. There are, of course, exceptions to the stereotype I will describe, but they are probably not the ones standing in your way.

The essence of the bureaucrat is that the System has given them a degree of power which they would not have, or deserve, under other circumstances. It is usually confined to a small area – which just happens to be the one in which you are interested. In the rest of their life they may have very little power and so what they have they exercise to the full. It reassures them that they exist – Descartes' phrase 'I think therefore I am' becomes 'I refuse therefore I am'.

Another distinguishing characteristic is that bureaucrats understand their function, but they do not understand the *purpose* of their function. The bureaucratic traffic warden concentrates on giving tickets, not on keeping the traffic moving; the bureaucratic office manager insists on clean desks and tidy files, rather than on the contribution their department makes to the business. They are not always fully to blame, of course, since they may be part of a system which demands bureaucratic behaviour from its officials.

TACKLING THE BUREAUCRAT

Two strategies present themselves for dealing with bureaucrats. One is the strategy of bring a higher power to bear. Carried out effectively it works because the abuser of authority tends to be very susceptible to greater authority. Authority is the bureaucrat's value, so they respect it. Later in the chapter I will return to this. But it is more satisfying, and a great deal more fun, for you as a persuasion player to use your skills to get the bureaucrat on your side. Your strategy is to use the troublesome characteristics which make bureaucrats what they are to get them helping rather than hindering.

Incompetence

It would be unjust to single out bureaucrats for their incompetence. It is a matter of observation that in any discrete group of people the ratio of incompetence to competence is roughly nine to one. Whether the group is composed of doctors or judges, street sweepers or traffic wardens, police officers or priests, the ratio remains constant. It may not be a coincidence that this is also the approximate ratio of followers to leaders in natural human groupings. Incompetence tends to be accompanied by obstinacy and a preoccupation with regulations; only in this way does the incompetent person feel safe. Using common sense or interpreting regulations flexibly requires a level of confidence which the incompetent does not ordinarily have.

So, you can be assured that nearly every bureaucrat who sets out to balk you blindly will be incompetent. Do not be fooled by educational qualifications. Education increases the ability of competent people; in incompetent people it merely removes what native wit they had and replaces it with second-hand notions.

Dealing with the bureaucrat directly

We have already noticed that bureaucrats express their ego through the exercise of power. Complementary to that is a high susceptibility to reactance (see page 173). Stand up to the bureaucrat's power and you ensure that they use it to the full. They cannot afford to do anything else, because they haven't anything else to do. Provided you can prevent the curtain of obstinate reactance coming down, you will find that they are extremely vulnerable to persuasion cards. They may be self-centred but they are rarely self-aware. Since they do not understand their own motives they can be easily helped to borrow the motives you have conveniently provided for them. Since their capacity for analysis is restricted you have every chance to get them to adopt the analysis which is important for your cause.

Look out for opportunities to make friends with the bureaucrat. It often takes no more than a smile or a chatty remark – preferably one that has an element of flattery in it. If you can establish some sort of human relationship before you get to the point at issue, you will have a good chance of success. It might be useful, for instance, to comment on the excellent choice of flowers in the receptionist's office before attempting to arrange an appointment. But complimenting a policeman on the shine of his car when you have just been flagged down may be better left until later in the transaction.

It is not impossible that there will be a rather obvious distance – at the general status level – between you and the bureaucrat. This can work both ways. Thrust your status at the bureaucrat and the smouldering fire of decades of disadvantage will leap into angry flames. Treat the bureaucrat as an equal and you may warm your hands at the glow.

A good phrase to remember is 'I wonder if you could possibly help me'. The atmosphere of that phrase is right. You are acknowledging the bureaucrat's power through asking for his help. And should you want him to break a rule, you must convince him, if only temporarily, that he is a warm human being with the breadth of mind to overlook the minutiae of the regulations. You are in fact raising the bureaucrat's Limited Image to a level which gives him the confidence to live up to the high opinion you clearly have of him.

The outcome of the transaction is favourable to both sides. You get what you want and the bureaucrat experiences the satisfaction of actually contributing to human welfare. Some day he may want to experience it again.

I have an elderly academic friend in Boston, USA who drives a battered car at inordinate speeds. He rarely uses his mirror because he is mostly looking at his passenger

> *to whom he is explaining his latest theory. When stopped by the police he says: 'Fifty miles an hour! Oh, officer, thank the good Lord you stopped me. I really had no idea. You know I could have done someone some real damage at that speed, or at the very least hurt myself. I do hope you didn't endanger yourself by trying to catch up with me . . .' And on he goes, until the policeman gives up and waves him on. The first time I witnessed this I thought he meant it; the second time I realised I had a very skilled persuasion player at the wheel. Nevertheless I try to avoid being a passenger in his car.*

Bringing force to bear

The alternative to charming the bureaucrat is to exercise your influence at a higher level. The most immediate way of doing this is through taking your case through any existing complaints or arbitration procedure which may exist. The problem here is knowing whether there is such a procedure and how to use it.

Sources of information

If you have an efficient local Citizens' Advice Bureau (CAB) you may well want to start here. But I prefer to get what information I can through relevant publications first. I will then quickly know whether the CAB has all the information about the particular problem I have.

> *CAB cannot be expected to be familiar with every problem thrown at them but they do have considerable resources. It was Kath Civil, manager of a CAB in Birmingham, who – dissatisfied with the results of the prosecution of three burglars – took a civil action to get a compensation order against them. Eric Bailey,*

> commenting on the case in the Daily Telegraph (5
> February 1993), pointed out that it restored to Kath
> Civil a sense of control over her life, which the burglars
> had threatened. Good for her!

Most large bookshops stock books which deal with the
procedures you need to use, but be sure you have an up-to-date
edition because the position can change quickly.

Which?, the magazine of the Consumers' Association, is
useful. In addition to the information in carries on products, it
tells you a good deal about services and the ways to get the best
out of them. Glancing at random through issues of the last
three years, I see articles on complaining, consumers' rights,
changing your general practitioner, dealing with medical
negligence, ombudsmen, banking rights, complaining to public
utilities – and many more. In addition there is the *Which?*
Personal Service which 'offers individual help and expert advice
if something goes wrong with goods or services you've bought'.
The address of the Consumers' Association is given at the end
of this book, together with similar organisations in other
countries. Many public libraries keep indexed issues of *Which?*
in their reference section.

Making complaints

If no complaints procedure exists you may have to complain
directly. But the first stage is to get your documentation right.
Keep bills, invoices and other documentation for any goods
and services you may buy; don't throw them away until you are
certain that you are satisfied. If you buy an item conditionally
– for instance, the shop agrees to change an amplifier if it
doesn't work satisfactorily in your sound system – get an
initialled note of this on the bill. If you write letters, keep
copies. Your letters should avoid any phrase which could be
used or interpreted against your interests. If you make
telephone calls, always ask for the name of the person you are
speaking to (if this is refused you may be sure you are talking to

a bureaucrat), and make a timed and dated note of the conversation. This is an instance in which pessimism is justified; assume that everything will go wrong and then judge whether your documentation is sufficient to prove your point. One day it may have to be.

It is not always easy to get bureaucrats to commit themselves on paper. A useful tactic is to write a letter afterwards, possibly using recorded delivery, in which you describe the oral arrangement. The letter is completed with the phrase 'Please let me know immediately if your understanding of what we have agreed differs in any way from mine'. Here, of course, you are using the bureaucrat's disinclination to reply to letters to make a record which they will find hard to repudiate later.

Initially you will probably have tried to sort out the situation at a low level, using the methods I have described above. But, if you make no progress, then take your complaint to the top. You may think that the chief executive is unlikely to be bothered with an individual complaint. Often you will be wrong, since many chief executives pride themselves on dealing with complaints. In any event, the person further down in the organisation, who may be asked to deal with the complaint, can never be sure that the chief executive has not read the letter and is interested in its outcome.

A very effective script for telephoning or writing to a chief executive goes something like this: 'I was rather surprised at not getting this little problem sorted out at a lower level. I know the public reputation you have for ensuring your customers are satisfied, so I thought I'd better get in touch with you directly. There's obviously been a failure in communication and some of your people aren't getting your message.' You will easily be able to analyse the programs which are being used here.

Publicity

The threat of bad publicity can often be an effective weapon. But you have to touch the right nerve. A large organisation may be concerned about television or newspaper coverage – particularly if criticising that industry is the flavour of the month with journalists; a local organisation will be more concerned with word-of-mouth publicity among its potential customers.

Remember the dangers of reactance. If you are trying to get the active goodwill of chief executives it is better not to threaten them at the same time; that can come in the next communication. You may, however, want to let them know, incidentally, that you would be in a strong position if you chose to go public. For instance: 'I notice that Tony Hetherington [a very competent journalist who deals with financial consumer complaints] was dealing with a very similar situation last week', or 'Having lived in Wimbledon for ten years a number of my friends mentioned to me that they had had a similar problem with other shops. But I have always been able to assure them that you gave excellent service.'

Your complaint will always receive the chief executive's attention if you happen to have, or have discovered, a personal connection. A letter which starts 'I hesitated before approaching you directly. But Jim Hammersmith, whom I believe you know, told me that you would want to hear about this personally.' Provided he does know Jim Hammersmith (and thinks well of him), you may be sure that your problem will get high level attention.

STRATEGIES FOR THE BUREAUCRAT

In studying the bureaucrat we looked for areas of self-interest in order to find clues to the motivation that might be used as a lever. In the bureaucrat's case it was a desire for the power to say no. But this principle can be extended by working on the assumption that a high proportion of the members of every group have chosen that way of life, not for what they can give, but for what they can get. If this makes the human race sound rather repulsive you may find it helpful to be ruthlessly honest about the real motivations which caused you to make the main choices in your own life.

- Use the self-importance a bureaucrat needs as a lever to get action by:
  — cultivating his friendship;
  — treating him as an equal;
  — using the phrase 'I wonder if you could possibly help me'.
- If this fails, take direct action making use of the proper complaints procedure.
  — You should have kept copies of all relevant documentation.
- If there is no effective complaints procedure, go to the top.
  — Assume the goodwill of the top person – appeal to his LIPS.
  — Publicity threats help, but use discretion.
  — A contact in common will assure attention.
- Just as bureaucrats have their own programs which you can use, so do other discrete groups you will encounter. Remember the power of the appeal to self-interest.

THE PRESSURE GROUP

Another weapon that can usefully be employed, if the circumstances are right, is the strength of numbers. I can perhaps illustrate this best through the story of the Lower Edge Hill and Darlaston Road Residents Association.

We live in a row of Victorian houses of an interesting architectural pattern. We were alarmed to discover that the owner of the next house intended to destroy the line of the row by pulling it down and erecting an apartment house in its place. Speed was essential as planning permission had been applied for and we knew the local council officers would be favourable to the scheme.

We talked to all the neighbours, pointing out to the weaker-willed that what was happening to us could happen to them next – and indeed more easily since a precedent would have been set. They undertook to write letters and we made sure that they did. We enlisted the support of the local historical society, who not only brought pressure to bear, but also instructed us how to handle the formalities. Then, with the strength of all these potential votes around us, we approached the local elected councillors – particularly those known to be interested in preservation. Being in an area where the council is finely balanced every vote was important.

When the planning committee sat, the council officers (bureaucrats to a man and woman, we suspected) recommended the scheme. Elected councillor after elected councillor opposed it and it was thrown out. It went to appeal and was thrown out again. It went to appeal to the Secretary of State for the Environment, but the strength of support and the quality of our documentation won the day.

By this time we had formed the association and had begun to be active in all matters which affected the

> *neighbourhood. Because we were energetic and effective, nearby roads asked to join. Now we are a powerful body, of four years' standing, with enough potential voting power to get every reasonable request we make. And because our newsletter lists shops and other services recommended by members of the association we seem to have little difficulty in ensuring that we get fair deals from anyone with whom we do business locally.*

Every pressure group will differ in detail, but there are some general lessons to draw from the account above.

- Energy is vital. There have to be some moving spirits who get going quickly and carry others through with their enthusiasm.
- While the initial problem particularly affected us, we had to find a motivation which would apply to other people. Our neighbours bore us goodwill, but why should they have taken action unless they saw that, at some time, their own interests would be affected?
- We knew the power structures involved. In this case it was the local councillors who were hungry for votes, as well as those whom we knew to be sympathetic to the interest we were protecting. In other instances the Member of Parliament might have been invoked, but, being a safe seat, this pressure was absent. And we suspected that the elected councillors might resent his intrusion from on high (reactance).
- We sought help from the experts – in this case, the local historical society. Our approach was facilitated because its president had taught one of our sons at school. They briefed us on the political situation, told us whom to approach and helped us with the documentation. And they also brought their own influence to bear.
- We capitalised on the original incident by forming a standing structure to continue the work. After the first stages, we moved ourselves into minor, background roles, in order to

emphasise that the association was for the good of all – and not a private benefit for us.

NEIGHBOURS

The Gospel dictum 'love thy neighbour' is more honoured, it seems, in the breach than in the observance. One advantage of getting to know your neighbours through a project like the one I have described is that reasonable, or even good, relationships have been set up before the demarcation or noise disputes have occurred. And inevitably they do; it is very hard to live cheek by jowl in a suburban street or in a block of flats without occasionally – if metaphorically – treading on each other's toes. But if you know and like your neighbour the liking program will help you to put the best interpretation on his actions, and to approach him in that light. The worst time to make someone's acquaintance is when you have come to complain.

Avoiding battles with neighbours

But, whether you know your neighbour or not, there are still some points to remember which will help you to avoid getting into the sort of battle that can only be resolved by legal means – a battle which usually involves everyone losing.

Stage 1

Use your imagination, and try and see the situation from your neighbour's point of view. Your neighbour may not even realise she is causing you a nuisance – and it is often the last thing she would wish to do. It may help to think about how you could have caused a nuisance unwittingly. Have you ever played the radio with a window open – without knowing what it sounds like when amplified into the garden, or walked across a wooden floor in heavy shoes? Have you ever clipped a neighbour's flowerbed with your car wheel or allowed smoke from your bonfire to smut someone's washing?

> *Philippa was telling me about a teenager nearby who was given to playing modern music with a heavy bass beat. When I pointed out that she had* Don Giovanni *playing at a good volume at the time, she said: 'But how could anyone object to Mozart?'*

Stage 2

Simply putting yourself into your neighbour's shoes may make you tolerant enough to bear the nuisance with patience. But, even if it doesn't, it will reduce the temptation to tackle your neighbour in fighting mood. The program between neighbours is, of course, reactance (see page 173). The noise, the smoke, the overhanging branch have invaded our territory – and territory is an emotional issue, as we saw in Chapter 4 when we were looking at NVC. Some ancient instinct makes us feel we are invaded and we are programmed to defend ourselves. Unfortunately our neighbour feels just the same: who is this person daring to tell me what to do in my own home? So escalation begins and it may not stop short of the law courts.

Count up to ten, or a thousand and ten – long enough to feel calm, friendly and benevolent. Then go and see your neighbour and, in an adult and tactful way which assumes he is unaware of the nuisance, explain to him how it affects you – and how much you would appreciate it if he could take action. Notice that you are leaving the matter to his goodwill (and he is a man of goodwill because you have treated him as such). Thus, you have made it possible for him to comply – and rather than losing face by responding he feels all the better for doing so.

Stage 3

If your neighbour is on a short fuse he may still react obstinately. No matter how provoked, do not respond in kind; contributing to the escalation makes matters worse. Leave courteously. Often your neighbour will feel ashamed of the outburst and quietly comply – perhaps after an interval to demonstrate that he is doing it voluntarily. If not, and the nuisance continues, then visit him again when things have had a chance to cool down. And use the same tactic. It is only when you have exhausted all these reasonable means that you should consider more formal action – remembering that this is a long and thorny path. But the need should be rare – after all, your neighbour is probably a reasonable person, just like you.

Which? magazine (October 1990) gives advice on noisy neighbours. If you have failed in the persuasion game described here your next move is a polite letter, of which you keep a copy, explaining the nuisance and asking your neighbour to desist. If this fails, your next recourse is your local Environmental Health Officer (EHO). EHOs vary in their willingness to take action, though they do have powers to prosecute. Failing this you can take the matter to the magistrates' court, but make sure you have kept a careful log of all the occasions of noise (or nuisance) and how it actually affected you. You can also take civil action and ask for an injunction. But this is a last resort and you should consult a solicitor first.

In 1993 a couple rowed so noisily and so lengthily that they each received a brief prison sentence. That must have been sweet balm for their neighbours' reactance.

THE NETWORKING PROGRAM

I have given two examples of networking in this chapter. One was the use of Jim Hammersmith's name when complaining to a chief executive and the other was our approach to the local historical society through its president. Networking is the art of building friendships or acquaintances in key places so that, whenever you want help, the personal touch can be used. It is often the key to success with beating the System − a source of information and a source of influence.

In previous centuries people could go around the globe with the appropriate letters of introduction and be received anywhere as 'one of us'. Today we do this less formally, but just as effectively.

Most people's networks are quite small. Each contact is a gateway through which you can pass to the next person, and the next person, until you are talking to the person who matters. Some people find it worth their while to build up an extensive network directly which, either through excellent memory or good records, provides the detail they need. They will make it their business to revisit the network frequently so that acquaintance is always quite fresh on the occasions that help is actually needed. Naturally their own good offices are readily available to members of the network so that the reciprocation program is fully in commission.

It was argued recently that women are at a disadvantage in the world of work because they do not have the same informal networks used by men. But this is changing and women's networks are springing up. Women have always had excellent networking skills in the domestic environment. It can get them local information and assistance in a way that any man would find hard to beat. The best networker I know is a woman who is involved in charity work; she knows everyone − and does not hesitate to use her social skills to get the very best out of them. Any woman who feels she lacks a good business network needs only to transfer her skills to the new environment.

> *Professor Robin Dunbar, in an article in* New Scientist *(21 November 1992) suggests that human conversation was primarily developed by women, who formed the core of primitive society. The women discussed the affairs of the group while men, more silently, conducted the hunt. If this is so, it would seem that women might have an evolutionary head start in building networks rather than any natural disadvantage.*

Networking is valuable because it cuts corners. The friend of a friend is already almost a friend, already some way along the path towards liking and trusting. It makes use of the fact that people are usually happy to do favours if it doesn't cost them too much. It makes them feel good. And, of course, a network of reciprocal obligations has additional power.

I suggested in Chapter 6 that being able to mention the name of a friend in the covering letter for a job application was a good move. This is a typical use of networking; it distinguishes you immediately from the grey mass of humanity. In this example, an employer contemplating a hundred similar applications for one job, with time only to interview a handful of candidates, will be likely to include the one which quotes a friend in common. This is an example of the endorsement program, a sub-program of networking.

When you are on the lookout for a new position, your friends, your siblings and your siblings' friends should all spring into action. Often they will hear of a new job before it has been advertised. Why post off a series of applications here, there and everywhere, when a telephone call or two can get you in front of a potential employer – and with a bit of influence on your side? Similarly, if you submit an article or a story to a magazine it may well get binned unread. With an introduction from the right person it stands out from the crowd. It may not get published but at least, unlike many others, it gets considered. But then skilled persuaders always arrange matters so that they stand out from the crowd; they are never anonymous.

Philippa had been suffering from stinging headaches which her GP had been unable to cure. In fact he had told her directly that she was neurotic. When her eyelid started drooping and she began to get double vision he at last agreed to send her to an ear nose and throat specialist to have her sinuses checked. He could find nothing wrong and suggested an appointment with an eye specialist – but none could be arranged for several weeks. She telephoned her optician; she knew him well because he had been a fellow student of an old friend of hers. He knew one of the best eye specialists in the area, who had looked after his mother; an appointment was arranged that evening.

The specialist took less than five minutes to conclude that it was not an eye problem but a neurological condition. Philippa mentioned that one of her oldest friends was a professor of neurology. A telephone call was made and, within an hour, Philippa was admitted to the best neurological hospital in London, and in one of the professor's beds. Luckily the damage to the nerves around Philippa's eyes was not irreversible. But it was many months rather than weeks before she recovered. If she had not taken control, and if one connection in that network had failed, Philippa could now be blind.

STRATEGIES FOR NETWORKING

- Build your network carefully; it may consist of a large number of people or fewer people whose own networks you can tap.
- Service your networks frequently:
  - keep in touch, if only through the telephone or by letter;
  - look for opportunities to perform favours for those in your network;
  - remember to be grateful – it makes your contact feel good.

- Women should make full use of their natural networking tools; they will often outpace apparent masculine advantages.

TRUSTING THE EXPERTS

As *Punch* said about getting married. Don't. At the beginning of this chapter I said that in any discrete group of people there will be nine incompetents for everyone that is competent. Philippa's story above illustrates this well. Her symptoms were, as the most elementary medical textbook would tell you, consistent with a ballooning of an artery in the temple, which can lead to a fatal haemorrhage, or – as in Philippa's case – an inflammation of the artery leading to nerve destruction. Neither her GP nor the specialist she saw had recognised the symptoms; the help she received was from the two medical people who had been identified as competent through personal connections.

> *Most of us, directly or indirectly, pay high fees to the investment managers who pick the shares in which our pension schemes and units trusts are invested. Unfortunately there is much evidence that they could do the job just as well by sticking in a pin. Or a dart. A Swedish newspaper is currently backing a chimpanzee against a number of top investment managers. He chooses shares by throwing darts. As at 8 September 1993, according to the* Daily Telegraph, *the chimp is well ahead.*

Doctors are just one group. We are aware of their failings because we use their skills frequently and in matters which are sometimes vitally important. It would have been as easy to tell you the story of the administration of an estate which took 20 years to finalise through a chain of legal incompetence. How about the bank manager or the financial adviser? They are no different from the garage mechanic who assures you that a vastly expensive repair is the only answer. In each case we are consulting people who represent themselves to us as experts, and often have the income and the trappings to go with it. And in nine out of ten cases they delude themselves.

> *Academic scientists tend to be hard on any alleged expert who does not advise according to objectively established facts. This gives a particular interest to an experiment in which 12 articles by eminent scientists were resubmitted for publication to the journals which had previously published them. The author was given a different (and unknown) name. Three of the journals recognised them as duplicates. Out of the remaining nine, eight rejected the articles. Following usual practice each article had been sent to two 'referees' – experts in the subject who were asked to comment. Every referee and every editor declared that the article considered was unfit to publish.*
>
> *Who was right: the original referees who recommended the articles when they had well-known authors or the later referees who rejected the same articles when they had unknown authors? Or are academic scientific experts no more reliable than any other expert?*

Need they declude us? Many people feel helpless in the hands of an apparent expert. After all we don't understand the subject or we wouldn't be going to an expert in the first place. And it seems offensive to challenge the opinion of this great person – they may become angry or we may hurt their feelings.

The persuasion player does not, of course, react like this. First of all, with the odds at nine to one against, you should regard the onus as being on the expert to prove his or her competence. Second, if the expert is angered or hurt by your scepticism, who has the problem? Certainly not you, the persuasion player. Third, you are paying the expert, either directly or through taxation. It is your body, your legal rights, your financial affairs that are being considered. So you had better be in control.

STRATEGIES FOR TACKLING THE EXPERTS

- Wherever possible, get an introduction to an expert from someone who has had experience of their services.
- Do what homework you can to understand something of the matter on which you are seeking advice. A little knowledge may be a dangerous thing, but it's a great deal less dangerous than no knowledge at all when you may be putting your life or your fortune into the hands of an educated idiot. At the very least, your knowledge of the subject should induce them to treat you as an intelligent human being.
- Prepare carefully. You may find it helpful to write down what you want to know. Keep it as a checklist – or you may only remember that important factor when the interview is over.
- Review Chapter 3 of this book, and remind yourself of how personal authority and credibility can be built on insubstantial foundations. Above that pin-striped suit a pin-sized brain may be lurking. The research shows that qualified professionals are generally inclined towards a greater confidence in their judgements than the evidence warrants.
- Ask questions. Ask all the questions you want answered, remembering that the questions you may feel the most embarrassed to ask are usually the ones to which you most need an answer:

  'Tell me, doctor, are you quite sure of your diagnosis? Are there any other conditions which have similar symptoms?'

'I'm glad to hear, lawyer, that you think we'd have a good case if we took this to court. Perhaps you could explain to me just why you think so and how you would judge the odds of success.'

'Tell me, financial adviser, just why you think this investment will do so well. What hard evidence do you have of its potential success?'

If the expert is unwilling to explain or is unable to make the position clear to you, you can assume that they are sailing under false colours. People who really know their subject understand it well enough to explain it and are normally glad to do so. Good doctors, in particular, will be familiar with the studies which show that proper explanations to the patient can contribute significantly to their recovery.

To some of the questions you will already have at least a partial answer. By obliging the expert to answer *your* questions you are sampling the breadth of the knowledge he has; what *he* chooses to tell you may be the sum of all he knows on the matter.

If you know nothing of the subject, you have all the more reason to ask questions. You are entitled to understand what is going on. While you may not be able to judge the correctness of the answers you get, you may well be able to form an opinion about the expert's competence from the way in which they tackle the questions. If you remain unsure don't hesitate to get a second opinion.

PERSISTENCE

Persistence could well have been added to the tips on tackling the experts. But I use it as a concluding section to this chapter because its application is general. People who ask questions, people who want to be treated as intelligent adults, people who want to get their reasonable rights and people who refuse to be treated as one of the dismissable mass can be unpopular. Incompetent suppliers of services, of all kinds, dislike them. But, when your cause is right, persist. As an individual with high personal authority you will never be discourteous, you will never lose your cool. But you will be firm and others will quickly realise that you are not to be trifled with. Control or be controlled – that is the basic rule of the persuasion game. And the persuasion game is the game of life.

Persuasion in the family

10

Persuading your partner

AFTER THE ORANGE BLOSSOM, couples have to come to terms with the reality of each other and negotiate a stable basis for a relationship. Is there really a difference between marriage and long-term living together? How do you play, or defend yourself against, the powerful cards of dominance and guilt? What are the skills of communication and the traps of bad communication about which counsellors teach their clients? Should you be honest in your relationships? Why do some people actually become increasingly incompetent as marriage progresses?

WHEN I was planning this chapter I asked my wife for some views. She was very interested. 'Will it explain', she said, 'how to get your partner to bleed a radiator or to keep his papers tidy?' I recognised the topics as ones of current interest in our household, but I had to explain that although this book as a whole contains programs and methods which may be effectively used for such persuasion, the very nature of marriage – being a long-term relationship – contains some programs that are intrinsic to it. Persuasion in the sense we have been giving it is incidental to marriage. Rather deeper programs need to be invoked in order to ensure that the necessary basis of stability is maintained.

THE CYCLE OF ILLUSION, DISILLUSION AND ACCEPTANCE

Love, they say, is blind. Our genes in their remorseless quest to replicate themselves have developed methods to ensure that our choice of partner is made on inadequate evidence. The familiar programs of attractiveness, liking and subsequent trust play an important part; and first impressions, bolstered by our belief that we are in control of events, help by suggesting that the goods in the shop window will deliver according to their promise. Similarity is important too, and marriage partners tend to share social backgrounds, geographical origins, basic value systems and even a rough equality of physical attractiveness. (We have noted the part that similarity plays in liking throughout this book.) Proust argued that the process of falling in love was one of projecting our own characteristics on to the beloved, so that we, in effect, fall in love with ourselves.

> *The reason why the similarity-equals-liking program has developed in our genes can be seen here. Stable relationships, needed for the care of the young, are more likely to be maintained when the partners are similar. So it is evolutionarily useful for us to like similar people.*

Not surprisingly the cloud of orange blossom which brings us to the altar is soon blown away by the rough winds of reality. We discover that our partners are not ourselves but genuinely separate persons with their own needs and ideas, that they have real faults and deficiencies. The benefits we expected from the married relationship begin to be equalled, or even exceeded, by the price we have to pay.

The outcome of this disillusion is a period of adjustment in which we try to come to terms with reality. We adjust our expectations, we negotiate aspects of the relationship, we become accustomed to the drawbacks and try to accept them. This process continues throughout marriage and is reactivated strongly by major changes, such as the starting of a family, which bring out new factors and require new adjustments. However, the first period of adjustment is most important because there is usually more to be done and, unless it takes place, the marriage will not continue anyway. It is no coincidence that the most likely time for marriages to end is after about six or seven years, and the period appears to be reducing. The problems which are never properly resolved at the beginning can be tolerated for a period, but eventually they cannot be sustained.

> *Somerset Maugham, the novelist, claimed that no couple remained in love for more than five years. And it's true that unless a relationship switches its basis from orange blossom to reality in the early years, even the orange blossom (which can waft around good marriages for half a century or more) must disappear.*

The healthy outcome for most relationships is that the partners accept that, although things are not perfect, they are 'good enough'. And the adjustment period may be useful in itself if it has given the partners the tools which are necessary to continue the renegotiations which the future will require.

> *The cycle of illusion, disillusion and acceptance (or non acceptance) of the situation as 'good enough' is mirrored in many human experiences. In relationships it can be seen in children who, one hopes, eventually find their clay-footed parents 'good enough' or, at a less emotional*

> *level, in friendships. It occurs when we take on a new job*
> *or buy a new car. It is a basic program which fools us*
> *into undertaking new ventures and then helps us to live*
> *with the practical consequences.*

In the course of this chapter we will review some of the tools for renegotiation and adjustment, and examine the programs which can help or hinder.

THE PACKED BAG SYNDROME

Getting married on the basis of inadequate evidence requires a leap of faith. It is not surprising that the rate of marriage breakdown makes people anxious to hedge the bet. One way of doing this is to have a metaphorical packed bag in the attic; if necessary one can pick it up and leave. This may show itself in insisting on the individual ownership of household items – this desk is mine, that picture is yours. If the marriage breaks up both people know what is theirs and has been theirs all along. Earnings belong to the individual and any equalisation of family income is by favour and not by right. The ultimate packed bag is when a couple, or one of a couple, choose a quasi married relationship whose lack of commitment symbolises their intention to leave when it suits them.

> *Quasi marriages raise difficulties of terminology. 'Partner'*
> *is being increasingly used, but it can cause confusion with*
> *business partnerships. At one stage 'POSSL-Q' (Person of*
> *Opposite Sex Sharing Living Quarters), taken from survey*
> *forms, seemed to making headway – but it excluded*
> *homosexual relationships. My preferred term 'Layby',*
> *which combines the idea of the temporary with the idea*
> *of the connubial couch, does not seem to have caught on.*

The packed bag turns the relationship itself into a persuasion game. The usual stake is the emotional investment of the parties; and the stakes may be unequal. Typically they are higher for women. The object of the game is to keep it going by ensuring that your own demands are not too great and that you meet the other's demands adequately. The stakes tend to increase, but the player who can keep his or her stake lowest has the edge. He or she can control the relationship and increase demands without having to raise their own contributions commensurately.

One problem of the packed bag approach is that most people have a deep need for security in their relationships. In many important ways marriage is a continuance of the parent–child relationship; that is, the spouses ask from each other a continuance of what their parents gave them by way of emotional security or they hope to receive what their parents failed to give them. The secure child is confident and independent; the insecure child is tentative and clinging. The packed bag is a symbol that Mummy or Daddy may always walk out on you, you can never feel safe and you can never trust yourself to the relationship.

Another issue is that the commitment of marriage begets a determination to solve the problems of adjustment. If you have to make the best of an unchangeable situation you have the motive to do so. But the existence of the packed bag provides an option which may mean that problems which could have been solved lead to a trip up to the attic and a telephone call for a removal van.

The choice is a difficult one: relationships do break up and the packed bag is a rational way of limiting the damage. Whether you regard that solution as pessimistic or realistic is up to you. On the other hand, full commitment in marriage gives the strength and motivation to overcome difficulties. Whether you regard that as optimistic or foolhardy is up to you.

It may be thought, and it is often claimed, that living together before marriage is a solution to this problem. That is, the experience and successful adjustments of cohabitation enable the couple to make a rational decision about the success of marriage when they choose it. This can be overtly a form of trial marriage – a game where the pay-off is marriage itself, if you pass the test. Unfortunately its ability to predict the success of marriage is illusory. The figures (Office of Population Censuses and Surveys) show that couples who marry after cohabitation are 60 per cent more likely to experience breakdown than the others. There may be different reasons for this, but one at least is that an uncommitted relationship and a committed relationship do not just differ in degree, they differ in kind.

A BASIC STRATEGY FOR MARRIAGE

- We are probably not much better at picking partners than we are at selecting candidates for jobs. But since basic similarities – such as shared value systems, interests in common and cultural background – correlate well with success, they are worth bearing in mind. It is no coincidence that a long-term friendship is also likely to show such similarities. No level of sexual attraction can survive the absence of the qualities of friendship between partners.
- No partners make an exact match – and disaster awaits those who expect this. Negotiation, adjustment – and the acceptance of the 'good enough' – are essential.
- Given the difficulties and dangers involved in building a lasting relationship, we have to decide whether to choose complete commitment – which gives the best chance of success and exacts the highest price for failure; or the 'packed bag' which limits both. You choose – it's your game, your stake, your life.

DOMINANCE IN MARRIAGE

The depth of our authority and obedience programs ensures that these play an important part in marital adjustment. In some cases the need for someone to be dominated or to dominate may have been the basis for the attraction which led to marriage in the first place. The game can, of course, continue – to the great satisfaction of both parties. The 'victim' may add to the psychological pleasure they receive, the satisfaction of feeling hard done by, and the sympathy they therefore receive from relatives and friends.

> *One wife came to counselling after a few years of marriage, complaining of her husband's physical violence. By bad luck she was allocated to the counsellor who had seen her while she was engaged. He reminded her that she had brought the same complaint even before she had committed herself.*
>
> *Physical bullying is predominantly male. Psychological and sexual bullying belongs to both sexes, and is much more common. But it is less recognised because the bruises are inside.*

Unfortunately this situation is inherently unstable. Lord Acton's dictum that all power tends to corrupt applies here and the caring exercise of authority in the early days of marriage may well slide into tyranny. The worm may turn if the balance becomes insupportable and this may be triggered by persuasion from outside sources. Often the victims 'grow up' as they mature and their wish to be dominated disappears.

Renegotiating the balance of authority is difficult. It is seen by the dominating partner as changing the rules of the game and therefore cheating. Some skilled players learn to obtain real control without their partner ever discovering that they have lost all but the illusion of authority. In fact, many healthy relationships subsist because of the ability of the partners to sustain each other's illusions.

Psychological accounting (see Chapter 2) plays a big part in the satisfactory adjustments of marriage. The compromises necessary to sustain the relationship become more bearable as the compromiser comes to believe that the new situation is what he or she really always wanted.

STRATEGIES FOR DOMINANCE

- The objective is to achieve the balance of dominance with which both can live; this can change at different stages. There is no ideal pattern, just the one that's right for you.
- The dominance pattern can be renegotiated, sometimes only within limits, by using the communication skills described below. In difficult cases a marriage counsellor may be needed.
- It may help to look for different areas of married life in which the different partners predominate. But beware of 'learned helplessness', described below.
- Remember that true control does not necessarily go with the appearance of dominance.

WITH THIS GUILT I THEE WED

Guilt is a high card in the marriage game. There is, of course, a healthy guilt which comes from having freely done something wrong and regretting it afterwards. It is expunged by putting the wrong right. Unhealthy guilt comes from perceiving that we have done, or are doing, something wrong – but it is

something over which we have no control. One therefore has
no capacity to put it right. Because a tendency to unhealthy
guilt is related to temperament, it does not have to be
consistently attached to a happening or a habit. It may be free-
floating; that is, an individual may have a general sense of guilt
which attaches itself to whatever apparent shortcoming is
readily to hand.

> *Regret for wrongdoing is a necessity for social living.*
> *Unhealthy guilt appears to be a variation on this and*
> *may have developed because it reinforced the tendency*
> *to submission which had a value in stabilising society.*
> *Some degree of unhealthy guilt is widespread, but an*
> *excessive tendency is often related to childhood*
> *experiences – for example, the child who was always*
> *blamed or the child who was always compared to a*
> *superior sibling. Unhealthy sexual guilt is frequently*
> *attributed to early upbringing, and reinforced by the*
> *strictures of parents, teachers and the church.*

The value of guilt in marriage lies in its power to *control* the
relationship. A husband can be made to feel guilty because his
job carries insufficient status or insufficient money. If he is
successful at work he can be made to feel guilty because he gives
too little time to the children or too little time to the jobs that
need doing about the house. A wife can be made to feel guilty
about going out to work, not making enough of her appearance
or neglecting household tasks. Both can be made to feel guilty
about their enthusiasm for sexual performance, whether too
much or too little. These examples demonstrate that guilt can
operate wherever we feel, rightly or wrongly, that we are not
matching up to something that we *ought* to be doing. 'Men
ought to be breadwinners, women *ought* to be nest builders.'
We may regard such roles as hopelessly old-fashioned; but we
forgot to tell our genes.

One might suppose that wives with full-time, high-flying jobs would be entitled to share domestic chores equally with their husbands. But a recent study, from Reading University, showed that such wives still undertook the heavy domestic work while husbands only paid lip-service to equal sharing. Men were described as only doing bits and pieces, and, when they did share, the wives still took overall responsibility. Many other studies have shown that equality in terms of responsibilities in the home is far from being achieved. While we may see this as a result of male oppression, it could scarcely be so widespread without female collusion induced by the guilt of not fulfilling their archaic role.

A clue to trumping the guilt card is contained in Chapter 3 where a characteristic of the dominant person is described as his refusal to take over the problems of others. He solves *his* problems, he leaves others to solve theirs. A strong tendency to unhealthy guilt leads directly to accepting problems which either properly belong to the partner or are simply a fact of life, belonging to no one but faced by both. However, we should bear in mind that the natural victim (see above) may actually find their guilt is necessary to them since it provides a number of psychological rewards.

A partner may also feel guilty about problems which emanate from them but which they are unable to solve. If, for instance, a husband does not earn enough to provide his family with the standard of living they need, it does seem to be his problem. But if this is because he is not able to change the situation then it cannot be his responsibility. You cannot be responsible for something which you cannot control. If he feels guilt, or has guilt imputed to him, the difficulty is only compounded. If a wife does not find it in her to turn into a raving sexual fiend thrice nightly her acceptance of guilt for what she cannot control is likely to make the situation even worse. This leads to a further twist in the spiral of guilt; you begin to feel guilty about feeling guilty.

Many marriage relationships are characterised by the playing of guilt cards. Sometimes one partner holds them all, sometimes they are shared equally. But they depend for their effect on the willingness of the other player to accept the guilt card. Those who are clear-sighted enough about who owns the problem, or who refuse to accept responsibility for what they cannot control, will render the card unplayable. It is as well to establish this early in the marriage; the situation is recoverable later, but with more difficulty.

LIMITED IMAGE PERFORMANCE SYNDROME

Guilt playing can often be the dynamic of a marriage; and may well be holding it together. But it is unstable and negative – leading to what one American sociologist described to me as a 'mutual disconfirmation cycle'. It brings about the gradual destruction of personality which kills the marriage or sucks the goodness from it. There are no winners. But fortunately there is a mutual confirmation cycle which does just the opposite. The LIPS player uses their cards to build up the other person by concentrating on what they can do rather than what they can't. (You will remember, from Chapter 7, that a boss is more likely to change behaviour by building on a subordinate's good points than on their faults.) Guilt paralyses or causes reactance. Developing one's self-image is freeing; it leads to constructive progress.

Marriage, I have suggested above, is a continuation of the parent–child relationship. Ideally our early relationship has left us with an inner sense that we are lovable, worthwhile people. In adult life we need our marriage partner either to heal any missing elements in

> *the picture or to sustain and strengthen it. A marriage which is built on the basis of raising LIPS is fulfilling its function; a marriage which is based on the playing of guilt cards is not.*

LIPS in marriage is not always an easy card to play. Leaving aside the strong temptation to use guilt cards – which are readily available and effective in the short term – some people are very resistant to taking on a better image. That is, the inferior picture of themselves formed by previous experience is one they are reluctant to abandon. Like a patched old jacket it has become more comfortable than a new suit. It involves less challenge and provides the excuse: what can you expect from someone as pathetic as me? Such people develop two very different ears. One is extremely sensitive – so sensitive that it can hear criticism faint enough to be undetectable by anyone else; the other is so deaf that it fails to pick up any approval or praise no matter how loudly it is shouted.

So, if LIPS is the counter to the guilt card, a determination to accept only guilt cards is a counter to LIPS.

STRATEGIES FOR GUILT

- Clarify, in relation to your own guilt feelings, between elements which you can put right because they are genuinely under your control (healthy guilt – constructive) and where they are not (false guilt – destructive). This will not change your false guilt feelings in the short term, but it's an essential first step. Remember *it is only your problem* if you are able to control the feelings or behaviour involved; otherwise, it is a mutual problem or your partner's problem – depending on the circumstances.
- It is very helpful to complete this exploration together with your partner, when you feel you can support each other not only in the discovery but also in the desired changes.

- Look, ideally together, at how and why you play guilt cards in your relationship. Recognising them is the first stage and action plans to correct them is the next stage. (See note on action plans at the end of Chapter 2.)
- The steps above help you to take immediate corrective action. Long-term improvement comes from raising each other's LIPS.

COMMUNICATING IN MARRIAGE

What would you see as the purpose of marriage preparation courses? Most people see them as opportunities to obtain information – about budgeting or house purchase, for instance, or family planning. While such information is important, the real purpose is to start the process of communication. That is, the couples are helped to explain and listen to the other explaining, how they feel about different topics that will be important to them.

One session might be devoted to thoughts about disciplining children. A couple may find that they have a very different approach to this and discover that it is related to their own experiences as children. Once they have understood how each of them has arrived at their present view, tolerance and acceptance become possible, and mutual discussion leading to modification can take place.

Few difficulties can be completely solved at such courses and many topics are not covered. But the aim is to teach a couple that their individual views are a product of their histories, that they can be talked about, and that good talking and listening is a habit they must take into marriage. One couple told me that, when driving to work together, they had always listened to the radio. Since the course started the radio had never been turned on – there was simply too much to talk about.

A marriage counsellor is faced by a wide variety of problems but in most cases teaching a couple how to communicate is a necessary part of the therapy. This might suggest that a failure to communicate is confined to marriages in trouble, but this is not so. Few couples are good at communication and this lowers the quality of the relationship. But their skills may be adequate for survival or they may be lucky enough to avoid the crunch points where good communication is essential.

> *David and Margarita had each become aware that something was wrong between them. They couldn't put a finger on it, but they felt less close, less friendly, more dull. After some months of this Margarita brought her feelings to the surface; David was surprised to find that her feelings were similar to his own. They traced their origin back to the time when David was promoted from the sales force into being sales manager, some time before. He had stopped working from home and now worked regular office hours. Margarita had felt excluded from part of his life which she had formerly shared and he, preoccupied by new duties, had not realised the effect. Once they both understood how the other felt, it was quite easy to make the necessary adjustments and restore full harmony.*

Creative communication

Good communication in a relationship is not measured by the number of words said but by the quality of the mutual exploration. It requires the speaker to explain how they feel in a direct way without any hidden messages that seek to persuade. Contrast these two examples:

> *'Frankly I feel neglected. Whenever I want to talk to you you're always too busy, you don't want to know. All you seem to need from me is three meals a day, the house clean – and a bit of bed. You'd be better off with a paid housekeeper.'*

'I feel lonely. There are so many things I want to share with you but somehow I never seem to choose the right moment. I get the feeling that you've lots of things on your mind which I don't share in. And I'd like to.'

The two statements describe the same sorts of feeling. But which is the most likely to lead into a row and which is most likely to lead to a constructive response?

The necessary complement to the good expression of feelings and difficulties is good listening. Again let's contrast two possible responses:

'Your problem is that you've got no resources. Here am I: out most of the day trying to earn a living and just when I want a bit of relaxation, I have you getting at me because you're bored.'

'Yes, I think I see. You want to talk about lots of things but I seem to be putting you off. Almost as if we were two separate people living in the same house. Is that it?'

The difference here is not simply a matter of the responder being tactful; it is a quite different way of listening. The first responder is not really listening at all, but noting the messages and constructing a riposte which will put the speaker back in place. The second responder is trying to understand how the speaker is feeling, attempting to see the situation as the speaker is seeing it. The time for a riposte, or rather a presentation of how the responder in turn sees things, comes *after* the responder has listened to and understood the speaker.

This is empathy in action. Sympathy and empathy are not the same thing. Sympathy means understanding feelings and sharing them. Empathy means understanding how a person feels, but not necessarily feeling in the same way or even agreeing with that point of view. The distinction is important because our natural reaction to a communication which is critical (or which we interpret as critical) is to shoot it down. We feel that sympathy weakens our position. But empathy doesn't. We don't know whether the second responder agrees with what has been said or not, we only know that he or she has listened fully and understands how it is for the speaker.

Empathy is the key to listening for three reasons:

- first, it means that our response is to what the speaker has actually said and not to our interpretation of it;
- secondly, once the speaker feels that their point of view has really been understood, reactance is lowered and it becomes psychologically possible for them to review and consider modifying their position;
- thirdly, the process of seeing things from the other's point of view leads to an understanding and a greater tolerance of it.

> *Creative listening is a skill whose lack has brought great sorrow to the human race. It should be taught in schools; managers, trade union leaders and politicians should undergo compulsory courses. Its absence triggers conflict in every sphere.*

Creative communication is very difficult. Even if we know about it and understand its importance, it is still too easy, even automatic, to load our messages with critical barbs. Similarly, reactance makes it all too easy to cut off our listening faculty and respond in similar vein. This becomes another twist in the mutual disconfirmation cycle, which, in extreme cases, ends in the counselling room. By this time the habit has become so fixed that the counsellor has to work very hard and over a long period to teach the couple how to communicate creatively. Fortunately the results of success can be very rewarding.

Total honesty in communication

It is sometimes thought that the basis of good communication is complete honesty and openness. But this is no more a recipe for success in marriage than it is in ordinary social relationships. We are seldom even honest with ourselves, let alone with other people. Of course, a couple may need to be frank and direct with one another in order to sort out a difficulty which is hurting their relationship, but with experience couples discover areas which are best simply ignored or avoided. They have learnt that trying to sort them out leads nowhere, and since the marriage is 'good enough' despite the differences, they can safely be pushed into the background.

> *In* Anna Karenina, *Tolstoy describes how Levin insists that his future wife read the frank diaries of his promiscuous bachelorhood. He is determined that his marriage should start off on a basis of ruthless honesty. Kitty is extremely distressed. For whose sake was he doing this, his or hers?*

Total honesty is a powerful card in the marital game. It can wreak destruction, induce massive guilt and create problems which are sometimes insurmountable. Yet honesty is a virtue – who can blame anyone simply for being honest?

Covert communication

I suggested above that it is only too easy to load one's messages with critical barbs. A barb has the feature of snagging in the wound; you can't pull the hook out because it's caught. If you say to me: 'I can't stand the way you leave the study so untidy', I can deal with that direct criticism. But if you say to me: 'I missed an important appointment because I couldn't find the papers in the study', I may be well aware that you are criticising me for my untidiness, but, put in that form, it's hard for me to deal with. After all you haven't made an accusation, only a plain statement of fact. You've got me hooked.

Covert communication, the indirect criticism, is a common card in marriage. It can run through all the circumstances of marriage, but the marital bed is probably the best arena. Few couples avoid playing it, for they enjoy their little triumphs too much. But each occurrence is a symptom of faulty communication allowing a point to be made without allowing the other an opportunity for dealing with it. The habit can easily get out of hand and some couples get to a stage when all their communication carries implicit, destructive messages. If they get to the counselling room before their relationship collapses, they will need to be taught how to give unbarbed messages about their feelings so that they can be dealt with in the open. Sometimes learning to abandon covert communication is all that is needed to get the relationship back on track.

> *When James and Maria went out in the evening, Maria was always late. Her last-minute preparations, which seemed to take so long, were Maria's way of showing how over-burdened she was with all her household duties. James had the engine running long before she came down and, when he drove them to their engagement, it was with much squealing of tyres and slamming of brakes. It made Maria gratifyingly nervous, but it was, or course, all her fault that they had to drive so fast.*

The counter-play is in principle straightforward. The creative listening response, exampled above, is one method. You simply respond as if the message had been given directly:

> *'You mean that my leaving the study untidy is really irritating you and now you've had an occasion when it's really held you up?'*

Alternatively, the situation can be brought into the open directly:

> *'James, I know you're driving quickly because I was late getting ready. I've got the message so can we slow down now, please?'*

In practice it is very tempting to respond to one covert communication with another, compounding the communication problem. Or we can accept the barb, and the frustration and guilt which comes with it. This is another habit which is best kept under control from the beginning of the relationship rather than attempting to deal with it once it is well established.

Learned helplessness

> *My wife is better at parking large cars than I am. She seems to be able to wriggle into tiny spaces and end up close to the kerb. When I am driving alone I am an average parker, but when I am with my wife my performance actually deteriorates. Under her patient, if occasionally long-suffering eye, I need to make several poor shots before I hand over the wheel and watch her zip it in in one. I have actually learned to be a helpless parker under those circumstances.*

The 'learned helplessness' program is not confined to marriage. Whenever two people are tackling a task together and one person is either acting as leader or is naturally better than the other, the second person is likely to deteriorate gradually in their ability to perform. The second person becomes less confident (lower LIPS) because of the contrast, and becomes more willing to hand over competence, and responsibility, to the other. However, marriage provides a playing field in which learned helplessness flourishes.

The program helps to explain why people tend to improve when others comment on their strengths rather than their weaknesses. It also explains why playing the guilt card is so destructive. Instead of spurring one's partner into mending their ways, it merely confirms, and thus increases, their inability to do so.

In the early stages of a relationship a couple will tend to share out roles in a complementary way – Maria is good with her hands so she takes charge of the DIY. James is good at figures so he looks after the money. But the effect of learned helplessness may mean that, over time, James becomes worse and worse with his hands, and Maria becomes more incompetent at handling figures. The skills and responsibilities become polarised, and sharing diminishes. The burden of marital tasks may develop unequally, but this will matter less at the practical level than at the psychological level. For instance Maria may be the repository of emotional understanding, relieving James of any responsibility for this, or James may become the repository for making family decisions in which it is assumed Maria is too incompetent to take part.

> *It is always said that men lack the ability to understand or express emotions; that's a woman's role. But time and time again marriage counsellors discover that a husband, once on his own, is able, with great relief, to express emotions he has concealed for years. Nor is his understanding of emotions necessarily one whit inferior to his wife's; he often has revealing insights which are quite invisible to her. Why is it so hard to open up and express feelings within the relationship?*

Of course learned helplessness must be distinguished from assumed helplessness – which is a common card. When my children were young I was able to change a Turkish towelling nappy, safety pin and all, at speed and in the dark. My grandchildren use the much simpler synthetic nappies; I am afraid I find I am quite unable to master the new skill.

STRATEGIES FOR GOOD COMMUNICATION

- Practise creative, or empathic, listening where you feed back your understanding of what you have heard – before you analyse or answer. It's a difficult habit to acquire and you may want to set aside specific time to develop your skills together.

- If your partner is unlikely to co-operate start by creatively listening to him or her. Very often the habit is learnt by imitation. But you will need patience.
- Use your discretion about areas which experience or exploration tell you cannot be changed – or cannot be changed at that stage. Once you have accepted this it is often possible to limit the damage by other adjustments.
- There are usually several topics which you can employ for practising empathic listening. Here are some examples.
  - Aspects of your personal histories which lead you to behave or feel in particular ways. Remember that, though you may not be responsible for your past, you are not a captive of it. Understanding and accepting your past is a start line for changing the future.
  - Covert communication. It is useful to explore how you both use it (be concrete, relate to actual examples); what makes you use it, how you can correct it.
  - Learned helplessness. Look at areas in your life where you have become less competent following marriage or where you are more competent in your partner's absence. Are there elements you want to correct; if so, how?
  - Discussing guilt feelings (above). It comes last in this list because it is reserved for those who are confident that they have already acquired some skills in empathic listening.

ACTION PLANS

Improving the ways you relate to each other in marriage is not simply a matter of good intentions. Indeed, the inevitable failure of good intentions on their own will often prove a block to trying again. Ingrained habits and deep feelings make change difficult. You will be greatly helped by an action plan. Turn to the end of Chapter 2 for some help with this.

11

Persuading your children

BEING A PARENT often causes conflict between keeping control and giving freedom. This chapter shows how the two are not incompatible if you follow the right strategy. You can start losing or winning the battle from day one. How will you cope with the 'terrible twos' and the 'awful adolescents'? How do you teach morality or the importance of rules? Why are systems of rewards and punishments potentially disastrous? If you are a less than perfect parent, does it matter, or can it help?

THE FUNCTION OF PARENTHOOD is to enable a child to develop from total dependency into an independent adult who can take their own place competently in the world, able to form and sustain good adult relationships. The challenge is one of managing the process of separation.

There is an apparent contradiction in this task. The parent's most immediate objective is to have a child who is well behaved and safe within the community of the family. Their persuasion skills, together with the battery of punishments and rewards at their disposal, indicate that they can be successful. But in the long run the child must be able to go it alone. That is, the socialisation the child receives in the family must become internalised so that it continues to influence the child in independent life. The objective is to maximise the child's internal and external freedom to make their own choices.

> *The deep program of deference to authority (Chapter 1) can lead to adults who will do abominable things under obedience. Parents can help their children to combat this program by teaching them to question orders and to maintain an independence of mind. But can they do this and have a satisfactorily obedient child at the same time?*

This chapter looks at the strategy a parent might pursue in order to achieve both these objectives.

The basis of the strategy is the belief that most children have a natural, internal direction towards becoming satisfactory human beings. At the same time they also have forces which draw them towards self-centredness, greed and selfishness. The parental task, carried out in different ways at different stages, is to guide and shape the child so that its natural good qualities predominate over its natural bad qualities. It is a matter of guidance rather than obligation because the development of the child must be internalised; that is, the parent is working to help the child to develop their own good nature, rather than imposing behaviours which are external to the child – and therefore abandoned as soon as parental power ceases.

Although the common cards in the persuasion game may have their temporary uses in the rearing of children they cannot be the answer to internal, and permanent, development. Persuasion is, of course, essential but, for the most part, the methods will be rather different. In this chapter we will look at some key aspects of child rearing to provide some examples.

A BUILDING PROCESS

Just as the physical development of the child is a building process, with each stage building on past development, so psychological growth requires that each stage needs to be satisfactorily accomplished in order for the next stage to succeed. A child should not be pushed too fast, but equally parents must hold themselves ready to help the child move on as soon as possible.

This chapter does not attempt to deal with situations where the failure of earlier stages creates special difficulties or where serious problems are arising. Professional help should be sought in such cases.

PERSUADING THE INFANT

The first two or three years of a child's life are crucial for emotional development. If all goes well the child has a basis of emotional stability that will be life-long; if the opportunity is lost or mishandled subsequent recovery may be difficult. The technique of inculcating emotional stability and high LIPS (see page 53) in the very young child depends on a natural device which continues throughout life, but is particularly powerful at the beginning.

The radar-equipped infant

In later life when the image we have of ourselves is reasonably robust, it is still modifiable by the reactions and responses of other people. We send out signals and people bounce them back; if the response is positive our image grows, if it is negative our image diminishes. The infant follows the same process except for the vital fact that he does not have an image to modify; he is wholly dependent on his LIPS in order to decide what his self-image is in the first place. And the primary people who bounce his signals back are his parents.

We know, for example, that it is important that people should grow up feeling lovable and worthwhile. The person who does not feel lovable will endlessly search for love in inappropriate ways and will never believe it when they receive it. The person who does not feel worthwhile is inhibited by guilt and restricted by his low LIPS from achievements which provide fulfilment.

Parents persuade their children that they are lovable and worthwhile by treating them as if they were. The child receives the signals which begin to define his image for him.

How does a child learn to be emotionally secure, with the resultant confidence and ability to trust people? Because the child's parents, by their presence, their reliability and their care, persuade the child that this is so. Sadly this is only too testable; many studies have related the absence of a secure parent figure in the early years to emotional problems in adolescence and adulthood. Confidence is visible early. The parent-deprived infant tends to be a clinger to whatever parent-substitute is available; the secure infant is prepared to roam and explore, because it knows that the parent will always be there when she or he is needed. The fully mature adult has an internalised parent, or rather the security of a parent, which he carries around with him. Of course, none of us is fully mature, but we can hope to approach it.

We have to face the fact that much of what we are persuading the infant about itself is not completely true. We have seen elsewhere in this book that characteristics like the leader's confidence that he can handle situations, or the optimist's belief that matters will turn out well, may be mistaken. We know that not everyone is to be trusted and that not all relationships provide emotional security. But, unless the child grows up with an inherent bias that this is so, he is condemned to failure. High LIPS may not be a perfect strategy for life, but it is the best we have available.

THE SOCIALISATION OF THE GROWING CHILD

The basic foundations of self-image and emotional security prove their value as later socialisation takes place. The strategy of persuading the child to internalise attitudes, values and behaviours continues, but now contains the added opportunities and dangers of dialogue. There will, of course, be particularly difficult times even with the most satisfactory child. The first of these occurs when a child is about two years old; this age is known as the 'terrible twos'.

BASIC STRATEGIES

- Your aim is to help your child to internalise right attitudes while maintaining acceptable behaviour.
- You must start the process of growing an independent adult from day one.
- A child learns the fundamental self-image of being lovable, worthwhile and secure from the way his parents treat him.

The terrible twos

This is a transformation stage when the child is leaving infancy and moving into childhood. It can be a shock when this darling little baby who has gurgled happily through infancy (for broken nights, ineradicable wind and teething are quickly forgotten) turns into an obstinate, screaming monster, showing all the characteristics of a miniature delinquent. Many a parent, shocked by a newspaper account of baby battering, has a little corner of their heart where they admit: there but for the grace of God...

If a two year old were capable of reviewing and articulating its feelings they would sound something like this:

'OK, the easy part's over. Up until now it's suited me fine to have Mum and Dad at my beck and call, tending to my every need. But they've run my life and now I want to run my own. I'm not a baby any longer, I'm a child. I'm going to be in control from now on. And have I got plenty of weapons! I can scream, that has a pretty immediate effect. Or I can whine − that really gets on their nerves. I'm big enough to wreak pretty fearsome destruction. I can refuse my food, and now I've discovered how much they want me to be potty-trained I've got real power.

'Of course my moods change a lot. A good deal of the time my parents are simply ogres; I hate them for the way they frustrate me − particularly Mum. On the other hand, there are times when I feel quite like a baby again − then, suddenly, I find I love them again. It's all very confusing. I'm not very happy. I wish everything would settle down.'

So do the child's parents. But the important thing for them to realise is that this is a necessary process of change, they have no more power to stop it happening than Canute had to turn back the tide. Their child is not being naughty but natural. Gritted teeth, heroic patience and opportunities to escape from the situation periodically are the fundamental recipe, plus the belief, so hard the first time round, that eventually it comes to an end and the sun will shine again.

However, there is a strategy to follow which makes life a little easier and, more important, enables the child to come through the experience more constructively. Because the child is trying to establish itself as an independent individual, the program invoked is reactance. It wants its own way and is intensely frustrated by anyone who interferes. It has to learn that sometimes it can have its own way and sometimes it can't. This is a hard lesson which a parent can assist by giving the child as much room to manoeuvre as is prudent, but equally by being firm when the bounds are about to be overstepped. And this is where confrontation occurs.

> *Escalation easily arises out of confrontation – as we saw in the matter of difficult neighbours (Chapter 9). The irony of war is that, for all its tragedy, it is psychologically no more than a child escalating a row with its parents or a pair of four year olds having a quarrel.*
>
> *Aeschylus' Oresteia is the great trilogy of plays, written more than two millennia ago, which suggested how man could escape from the cycle of revenge (reactance) and solve his differences through civilised means. It was playing in London, at the National Theatre, during the Falklands War.*

A battle of wills, where parent and child face each other in an escalation of anger in which it is sometimes hard to tell who is parent and who is child, happens to everyone occasionally. But it's unhelpful. Having made it clear that a second ice-cream is not on the cards, argument about the matter serves no purpose. Refuse to join the child's game of escalation and become skilled at finding exciting distractions. Because the child's rage is normally focused on the individual who has caused the frustration, the other parent (or granny or aunt) who, on this occasion at least, is guiltless by contrast can often help by being the distracter.

Parents often debate the smacking versus non smacking issue. The debate is somewhat academic because even the most idealistic parent can be provoked in a moment of temper into giving a smack. Fortunately it does the parent little harm and may even relieve some tension. It doesn't make the slightest difference to the child whose strength of feeling at that time well exceeds the minor smart of the smack.

In fact children at this stage are much more susceptible to parental approval or disapproval than they are to orthodox punishment. So the parent, however irritated, however recent the last incident of infant destruction, must always be ready to receive the child with love at the moment the child turns towards them. The child can turn the lines of communication on and off; but the parents must always keep their end open.

The awful adolescent

This chapter does not deal with adolescence in any detail: it is too big a subject to describe adequately here. But it is interesting, and possibly helpful, to realise that adolescence is only the 'terrible twos' somewhat magnified. The adolescent is going through a second inevitable process of accelerated transformation during which they are uncertain, unsettled and often unhappy. There is the same tension between freeing yourself from the hated parents, yet needing the loved parents. Adolescents have even sharper weapons, because there are more ways in which they can do themselves harm and have therefore more powerful emotional blackmail to hand.

Parents have to use the same gritted teeth and heroic patience as with the terrible twos. They must avoid confrontation, accepting that because they must protect their fledgling it will often occur. Above all, just as they had to do for the child years before, they must keep open the lines of communication from their end despite every provocation. And they will find it hard to believe that out of this cleansing fire which burns both parent and child a satisfactory adult will be born.

Reactance

We have met the reactance program in other contexts such as negotiation or in communication difficulties between husband and wife. But, like so many unhelpful adult responses, reactance is at its strongest in childhood – although the consequences, such as employment conflicts or war, tend to be more serious in adult affairs. Characteristically, the antagonists get locked into a cycle of reactance from which their pride does not let them escape.

Children need to learn how to minimise their own reactance, and this is done through good adult example and through the good handling of reactance episodes. This is not easy because the parents' own reactance may be called into play by the incident. Young children and adolescents are often frightened by their own anger and simply do not know how to get out of the hole they have dug. They need strong reassurance that they are loved and to be shown a ladder for climbing out. When all else fails a sustained hug can be remarkably effective.

STRATEGIES FOR THE TERRIBLE TWOS AND THE AWFUL ADOLESCENTS

- Understand how your child feels, even if he can't express it.
- Draw on your patience and faith that it will end.
- Avoid escalation of conflict by:
  - giving your child maximum room to manoeuvre;
  - if your child oversteps the limits don't argue; be firm;
  - looking for distractions – the other parent, perhaps;
  - the big hug is sometimes the only answer.
- With appropriate amendments adolescents are the same.
- In both cases, no matter what, keep your lines of communication open.

THE FOUNDATIONS OF REASON

It may seem strange to watch a parent with a very young child giving reasons for her instructions. For instance, 'Don't throw your food on the floor, it'll get dirty.' At, say, ten months a child doesn't understand the words and in any case is unable to follow this kind of reasoning. But the tactic is a good one. Over a period of perhaps years the parent is teaching the idea that behaviour has reasons and therefore consequences. The child is not being taught that behaviours are naughty in an arbitrary way – which quickly develops the dangerous obedience program – but that there is a reason for the rules. On this foundation the ability to question reasons can be built in later years.

The moral sense

It might be thought that this ignores the moral sense. But the understanding that there is a difference between right and wrong does not come from the parents, it is innate in the child. The parents can draw attention to it, and guide it, but they cannot provide it because it is part of what being a human is. When a mother says, 'Don't hit your little brother with your doll, it makes him unhappy', she is teaching a moral lesson. Of course the small child is unable to grasp the moral point, but when the child's own moral sense has developed sufficiently the lesson will form part of a pattern which – to the child – has always been so.

> *When one of my daughters was a teenager she was attacked in the street and mildly damaged. The police sergeant explained to her that the assailant's parents had never taught her that hitting people over the head with telescoped umbrellas was wrong. To which my daughter replied: 'I didn't know it was something one had to be taught. I thought people just knew.'*

Helping a child to be aware of its moral sense, and to direct it rightly, is a delicate task. At the early, pre-moral stage, the child's sense of right and wrong is defined by parental approval and disapproval. What power the parents have! They can warp the moral sense so that the child becomes guilt-ridden or intolerant of other people. Later they can make morality a system of arbitrary rules. If they are within a religious tradition they can even foist the responsibility for the moral obstacle course on God. In these ways, and often with a sense of satisfaction at a job well done, they can turn out people who will be moral pygmies for the rest of their lives.

Alternatively they can sensitively guide a child, as each stage of moral ability grows, to develop an intelligent sense of right and wrong which does not depend on rules but on reason. Their first means is by imitation; they model moral behaviour and the child's natural moral antennae recognise it for what it is. They develop the child's moral muscles by explaining reasons and later by encouraging a child to reason back. And the radar will still be working: no child can respect himself, his parents, or others — unless he has first been respected himself.

> *Some religious people may believe that morality through reasoning rather than commandment is to leave God out of it. On the contrary. Who gave human beings their innate sense of morality? Who gave human beings the power of reasoning with which to make judgements? Who provided a model of the practical meaning of love and invited, but did not oblige, human beings to imitate it? If you are a believer you will see God at the heart of a rational morality.*

None of this is easy to do. I have yet to meet any parents who can claim to have given their children an ideal moral example or who have felt that they had carried out moral education adequately. Fortunately children are very resilient and will survive parental incompetencies, provided that at least the direction is right.

What happened to rules?

This approach to rational morality does not exclude rules. Rules are not intrinsically moral. Driving on the left-hand side of the road (or tidying your bedroom) is not a moral question in itself. Any morality which is present comes about because breaking the rules has an effect on people. Every community, including families, has to have rules, but these should be as few as are necessary, intelligently thought out and consistently applied.

Children naturally resist rules, particularly a new rule. But it is surprising how quickly, provided parents stick with their decision, the rules are absorbed and then taken for granted. One can often see children insisting on their visiting friends keeping the same house rules which they themselves resisted only days earlier.

There is, in fact, a danger of children becoming too rule-based. A morality which is founded on rules is natural at a certain stage of development. But parents should look to opportunities to help them to understand the reason for rules, to see why circumstances may change them and to accept that sometimes they may be suspended, for a birthday, for instance. In this way the dangers of entering adult life with an unquestioning response to rules and a fully-fledged obedience program will be reduced.

Consequences

Consequences are what distinguish rules based on reason from rules based on arbitrary dictatorship. And a good method is to base disciplines as far as practicable on consequences. 'We don't start tea until toys have been tidied away' is more effective than 'Tidy your toys away because I say so'. Of course there is no intrinsic reason why tea should have to be dependent on tidiness, but the habit of relating behaviour to consequences is an important one to start early. By the time a child is old enough to debate the point, it has already internalised the relationship.

Meanwhile, one may hope that the toys have been tidied away without too many moans, that the young have settled into bed early to ensure time for a story at the third request rather than the tenth, that the homework has usually been done – so that the television can be turned on. If these were the only

benefits gained through the consequence method, many
parents would be grateful for this alone.

> *Rowena was a poor eater, and skinny with it. While her*
> *sweet tooth attracted her to cakes, pudding and ice-*
> *cream, she refused to eat anything 'sensible' to give her a*
> *balanced diet. The very thought of meat and two veg.*
> *brought on something near hysteria. Her parents were*
> *really quite concerned. The cure was to point out that*
> *the second course was dependent on eating the first*
> *course. She was in no way criticised, the connection was*
> *matter of fact. Initially first courses were made minute,*
> *and the puddings were magnificent. She resisted, then*
> *realised the connection was inevitable, and decided to*
> *give it a try. It took six months to establish balanced*
> *eating habits thoroughly. Now she can consume a pork*
> *chop and a mountain of chips without flinching, or*
> *affecting her slim figure. Her own baby daughter, I'm*
> *glad to see, faces food with the ruthlessness of a*
> *mechanical shovel.*

The consequence method reduces reactance because it is not
based on a battle of wills but on reality. If you run down a hill
too quickly you will trip up and hurt yourself. It is not a great
moral drama but a matter of fact. Robert Ingersoll, an
American agnostic, wrote, 'In nature there are neither rewards
nor punishments – there are consequences'. A child who has
been persuaded to look to the consequences of his choices from
an early age will take into adult life not only the habit of
making choices rather than having them made for him, but will
also be accustomed to thinking realistically about the
outcomes.

Rewards and punishments

However right Ingersoll may have been about nature, parents
are inevitably faced from time to time with shaping children's
behaviour by rewards or punishments. Operating the system of

matter-of-fact consequences I have described is a good running basis, but it does not deal with the crisis points. When a child who is determined to burn down the family home with a box of matches has the consequences explained to him, he may find the prospect rather appealing. The child's parents will need to bring the consequences much closer to hand – sometimes literally.

At first sight it seems strange that big punishments and big rewards are so ineffective in controlling children's behaviour. But we have all watched the 'smacking mother' in operation and seen how the effect is often the very opposite of what she intends. And it certainly does not follow that a child who has been brought up in a very strongly disciplined household behaves better either in childhood or in adulthood, though he may repeat the pattern with his own children.

The reason lies in a program which tells the brain, of both adults and children, that the higher the reward or the graver the punishment the less the behaviour in question is worthwhile for its own sake. If I promise a child a big present like a bicycle provided he does his homework regularly, he will say that he is conforming to get the reward. But if the reward is much less – let's say I'll take him to a football match – he is more likely to be convinced, through psychological accounting, that regular homework is good for its own sake, since the reward is clearly not adequate on its own.

Similarly, if I apply some heavy punishment because my son has beaten up his little sister, I teach him nothing about the virtues of kindness but only about the dangers of being caught. Several studies have shown that regimes of heavy punishment and heavy reward lead to worse rather than better behaviour. This suggests a strategy in which reliance on punishment and reward is avoided wherever possible. When it is needed, as it surely will be, both punishment and reward should be kept to the minimum required – leaving the maximum room for the child to make the desired behaviour their own.

> *When our children asked for an expensive present or to go on a school holiday trip we assented, if we felt it could be afforded. But the child would be required to make a contribution by saving from pocket money. Although the contribution was nominal in our terms it was important in the child's terms. The child demonstrated his commitment to his objective and when he got his heart's desire he knew he really owned it.*

However, the one reward which continues to have effect is parental approval. But while it should be ready and generous it should not be indiscriminate. Approval for everything soon loses is value. So parents should use explicit approval to build on good points or improve on weak points, gently shaping the child in useful directions.

It's not fair!

However careful parents may be, the child's strong sense of justice causes the cry of 'It's not fair!' to ring throughout the land. I have no evidence beyond my own experience of the value of the tactic I used. I simply pointed out that life was not fair and they'd better learn it in their home before meeting it in the outside world. I am now amused to hear my children telling their own children that life is not fair. I have either benefited or damaged at least two generations of children through using this statement. So I take no responsibility if anyone else wishes to adopt the same tactic. I can only tell you that it is very effective and that no child has yet thought of a good answer.

Extending choice

Most of us are caught between wanting to make our own decisions and wanting to be relieved of responsibility by depending on the decisions of others. It is important to help children to develop their own decision-making powers. Look for opportunities to give children choices wherever this is possible.

Giving children an opportunity to make choices is a useful way of calming reactance and nurturing early independence. A study with older children illustrating this was carried out by psychologists who secretly observed them playing with toys and noted which one they preferred. Later the children were given their preferred toy. But in half the cases the child was asked to make a choice, in the other half they were simply told they were going to get what the psychologists had observed was the preferred toy. The children who were given no choice soon gave up playing with the toy; not having chosen it themselves was more important than its attractions.

Of course choice must be graded according to the capacity of the child. At first the choices will be very simple and confined to minor matters. Later, when they are able to cope, it is a good habit to respond to their questions by asking them first what they think the best answer is. This can be aggravating, and I remember my 15-year-old son saying to me: 'Whenever I ask you what I should do, you always say, what do *you* think. Why can't you be like normal parents and just tell me?' But of course when I told him he never took any notice.

REFLECTING ON THE STRATEGY

I am aware that in the hurly-burly of child rearing the strategy I have rather baldly described sounds idealistic. Parents often feel they are surviving from day to day; they have no time for strategy management – only crisis management. What is more, they are aware that they make many mistakes – they are not perfect people. What I am talking about is an attitude of mind – a general approach which, however far we fall short at the tactical level, broadly informs what we are trying to do. I would summarise this as first building, and later reinforcing, a good level of emotional security and high LIPS, followed by midwiving a gradual development of independence measured according to the child's growing capacity.

Here are some further considerations which may console you.

- Perfect parental behaviour, if ever achieved, would in fact be detrimental. Children have to learn that the parents they know to be good people, and whom they love and trust, can also behave badly. If they do not discover this while they are young they will not be able to sustain adult relationships in which acceptance of the other's faults is essential. Nor will they be able to forgive themselves for their own shortcomings. Perfect parents are too heavy a burden for anyone to carry.

- A child who is never naughty will find it hard to mature. Part of growing up is to discover the boundaries of behaviour by trying to force them outwards. For the same reason the parents who do not maintain the boundaries of behaviour deprive the child of learning what the boundaries are. Adults will often tell you that they interpreted their parents' lack of willingness to check bad behaviour as a lack of care.

- Each child is a unique combination of ancestral genes. Parents are only partially responsible for how their children turn out. This thought can give much relief. It also means that it is quite natural to *like* one child more than another – which does not, of course, justify preferential behaviour. And every child will be thoroughly dislikable from time to time – just as every marriage partner is.

- If you have brought your children up to develop internal freedom, don't be surprised if they use it. A child with free will becomes responsible, later, for his own choices. You may not like the choices but they are *the child's*. You may continue to support a child while disapproving of his choices and certainly without feeling guilty about them. They have become their problem, not yours.

- Children are tough. They can survive far more parental damage than one might think.

ONE DAY IT WILL ALL BE OVER, OR WILL IT?

Parents look forward to the time when their children are grown up, settled and perhaps producing grandchildren. They are right to do so; it is a wonderful time. But it is never completely over – the umbilical cord has a long stretch. One of our daughters said to us the other day: 'Why do you continue to worry? Your children are all married, they're somebody else's responsibility now. And the grandchildren have their own parents to worry about them. You can feel free.' So she still has something to learn.

STRATEGIES FOR THE DEVELOPING CHILD

- If you want to produce a rational adult give your child reasons – even before they can fully understand them.
- Your child has an innate moral sense; your task is to guide and shape not to distort.
- Have as few rules as possible, but stick to them. Teach your child that rules are only moral questions in so far as they help or hurt others. This can include the general welfare of society and the family.
- Help your child to learn about consequences through experiencing them. Too much protection ultimately damages.
- A heavy reward and punishment regime will only work in the short term. But a sensitive use can maintain discipline that will work in the long term.
- Realistically you can only have 15 or 16 years to help this bawling bundle to be able to separate from you completely, as an independent adult. So maximise your child's growing independence, stage by stage. He may never thank you, but whoever said that life was fair?

12

Compendium of programs

THROUGHOUT THIS BOOK we have encountered programs. That is, a series of automatic responses which our brain uses to do our thinking for us. They are invaluable to you as a persuasion player because you can call up in your opponent's mind the right program to get the response you want.

IN THIS CHAPTER I will summarise the main programs described in the book; the Index of Programs will show you where you can find more information. Programs are interconnected and, very often, a particular persuasion ploy will draw on two or more programs at once. But, for the sake of simplicity, I will only show some of the more obvious connections by reminding you of the major programs and relating them to their important sub-programs. Major programs are in bold type; sub-programs are in italics.

RESPONSE TO CHANGE

This is the method whereby the brain and nervous system has evolved to react quickly to changes in the environment. This obliges it to arrive at judgements on the basis of incomplete evidence.

An example of this is the *first impressions* program – important, for example, for starting an interview or a speech, making a sale, establishing yourself as a leader or even falling in love. *First impressions* – good or bad – tend to persist despite subsequent, contrary evidence.

The *prominence* program is related to **response to change** because it gives disproportionate importance to information which stands out because it is recent or dramatic. The persuader can use ideas prominent in the opponent's mind (and the persuader may even have ensured they are) as a lever for their influence. A specialised *prominence* program is the *motivational story*. Because it enlists the imagination it carries impact which can be more persuasive than, for example a relevant statistic.

Because of our **response to change**, variety is a useful way of reviving attention in, for example, platform speaking.

Stereotyping belongs to this family of programs; we make assumptions about individuals because they belong to a recognisable group which we associate with particular characteristics. Similarly *language* programs make use of words which carry emotional (favourable or unfavourable) connotations. Their value lies in the fact that the listener is usually unconscious of the effect this is having on their judgement. *Non verbal communication* (*NVC*) is much more than a program, but we note here that much of its power lies in the fact that people are also influenced by it unconsciously and therefore form conclusions without bringing their rational judgement to bear.

THE COMPARISON PROGRAM

The **comparison** program depends on **response to change** but it is a major program in its own right. Because human judgement works by comparing new information with existing information – rather than working from scratch – the persuasion player has a powerful card available. By giving their opponent the basis against which to make the comparison (for example, by the use of *prominence* or by changing their *frame of reference*), they control the conclusion to which they will come.

The **comparison** program can work both ways. Thus, by presenting change in small steps, the degree of change can be concealed – and become acceptable. The use of *analogy* as a stepping stone to a new idea is another way of reducing the impact of change. So can *frame of reference*.

Comparison plays a part in many other programs because it is so fundamental to human judgement.

LIKING

Our programmed response to liking someone is to find them credible, trustworthy and therefore persuasive. *Attractiveness* is the first program we might think of there, and it operates most readily at the level of *first impressions* – which is quite sufficient for many persuasion moves. But **liking** goes beyond formal attractiveness and tends to last longer. Good NVC, or establishing *similarity*, perhaps of interests or experiences, contributes to liking, and seems to be an important factor in sustaining relationships. So does the *reciprocation* program, whereby we create debt which we can redeem later (see **guilt** below). The exchange of gifts and favours are formal ways in which friendly relationships are signalled, and can often bring them about.

Liking is a fundamental element in the *networking* program through which we make use of our contacts. They help us because they like us. This can also involve **liking** by proxy – when one contact passes us on to their own friends. This is a subsection of *networking* – the *endorsement* program. 'A friend of yours is a friend of mine' translates into 'anyone you like is someone I like, and therefore will be ready to trust and help'.

CREDIBILITY

Credibility is an outcome of **liking**, but other programs contribute to it. *Similarity* induces **credibility**, and so does establishing *qualifications* and *information opposed to one's own cause*. **Personal authority** is likely to be a big factor in **credibility**; it can be powerful enough to swamp the other programs.

PERSONAL AUTHORITY

Personal authority, or the quality which calls forth obedience and respect on the basis of the personality of the persuader rather than any explicit power, depends on the *obedience* program. This is the innate tendency we have to respond to the appearance and show of authority, and is one of the most difficult programs to counter. There is a whole cluster of *NVC* programs which are capable of communicating **personal authority**: *height and carriage*, and the use of *gaze, clothes, relaxation*. There are characteristic behaviours too, such as *defining the social situation* and the *refusal to take on other people's problems*.

Personal authority programs are hard to sustain unless we have a strong internal image which gives us the confidence that we are naturally in charge and know what is the best thing to do. We can assist ourselves in this by using programs for auto-persuasion: *mixing with successful people* to benefit from the positive aspects of the **herd** program (see below); *focusing on past successes*, which employs the *prominence* program; and *Couéism* – another use of the *prominence* program – in which the repeating of a confidence-building phrase gradually inserts it into the subconscious mind.

The **limited image performance syndrome (LIPS)** is the

program which induces us to act in accordance with how we feel about ourselves. The **personal authority** programs, above, contribute to raising our image. But **LIPS** is important in many other areas, such as **guilt** or *learned helplessness* – a program through which the competence of our associates actually damages our own performance. We may also sustain **LIPS** through the *illusion of control*, through which we prefer to believe that we are responsible for good outcomes and not responsible for bad. **LIPS** is not only valuable to us, it is also a program we can use to raise the performance of others. It can manifest itself in the personal programs of *optimism* and *pessimism*. We might notice here the importance of inculcating high **LIPS** in the growing child.

GUILT

The tendency to blame ourselves and to feel that we are in debt to others is a negative program which most of us share to some extent. It corrodes good self-image and endangers *refusal to take on other people's problems* by fooling us into thinking we have inappropriate responsibilities. It is damaging to relationships which are particularly dependent on good image, such as marriage. We can even feel guilty about feeling guilty. **Guilt** is often employed by 'hard sell' persuaders, especially in the charities field. Notice that a major counter to **guilt** in ourselves and others is provided by **LIPS.**

Reciprocation is valuable in the **liking** program (see above), but it also depends on creating a sense of obligation in which **guilt** plays a part. It can often be part of the bargaining process – in social transactions or formal sales and negotiations.

FEAR OF LOSS

Fear of loss is the program whereby an item becomes more valuable when it is in short supply. We see it most immediately in buying and selling when the discovery that 'this is the last in the shop' transforms our willingness to buy, but it also applies in many non commercial situations. It can relate to *attractiveness*, when the perceived attraction of members of the opposite sex can rise or fall according to their number in a mixed group.

CONSISTENCY

Our wish to appear consistent both to others and to ourselves is a powerful lever in persuasion. We use *psychological accounting* to rationalise inconsistency and the persuader will be quick to suggest this. *Psychological accounting* is also active in the *reward and punishment* program; this indicates to us that if we receive high rewards and grave punishments we should be motivated by these, rather than the nature of the behaviour itself. It is at its most obvious with children, but it applies similarly to adults. Changing *frame of reference* and *analogy* are often used for *psychological accounting*. *Commitment*, a related program, makes use of our need to fulfil our commitments. *Low ball procedure* is the deliberate use of commitment by the persuader when they increase the level of commitment by small steps. Encouraging our opponent to believe that they, rather than we, are responsible for an idea assists *commitment*. This also contributes to countering the **reactance** program.

REACTANCE

Reactance might be described as negative program because the aim of the persuader is to avoid activating the irrational obstinacy which we feel when we are over-pressed or our backs are against the wall. The *please and thank you* program stands for all the methods and phrases we use to give the impression that our opponent is free to make their own decision.

A subtle counter to **reactance** is *creative listening*; this has the power to reduce the tension and relieve the obstinacy – leading to the restoration of harmony.

Reactance has a positive version. An opponent may be challenged into action by suggesting they are incapable of it or their **reactance** against an idea which the persuader wished them to avoid may be cultivated.

HERD

The **herd** program is derived from our archaic need to base our safety and our values on what everyone else is doing. It is one of the most common programs and contributes to many others. It is also extremely powerful, governing our behaviour in many different ways. For this reason persuaders will use it often and work hard to reduce its impact on themselves. Like most programs it has positive as well as negative aspects; for example, we learn to become socialised through the *imitation* program – whether through watching our peer group or our parents.

Useful reading

General background

Berne, Eric, *Games People Play*, Penguin, Harmondsworth, 1964.

The original analysis of psychological games playing which started a whole movement in the understanding of relationships.

Carnegie, Dale, *How to Win Friends and Influence People*, Heinemann, London, 1986.

No one has written better on the whole subject. Carnegie has changed many people's lives; he could change yours.

Cialdini, Robert C., *Influence, Science and Practice*, Scott, Foresman, Illinois, 1988.

A serious study of the field of persuasion, but a most enjoyable read as well as highly informative.

de la Bedoyere, Quentin M., *How to Get Your Own Way in Business*, Gower Press, Aldershot, 1990.

A leading communications consultant described this as 'the most educationally rewarding book on human skills I have ever seen.' I am much too modest to agree with him.

de la Bedoyere, Quentin M., *Managing People and Problems*, Gower Press, Aldershot, 1988.

Available in paperback, this book is about practical ways to help people change their behaviour.

Machiavelli, Nicolo, *The Prince*, Rome, 1532.

If Socrates is the patron saint of persuasion Machiavelli is his first modern disciple. Always available in paperback somewhere.

O'Keefe, Daniel J., *Persuasion, Theory and Research*, Sage Publications, London, 1990.

This is an advanced students' text, but well worth the effort if you want to assess the evidence for persuasion techniques.

Sutherland, Stuart, *Irrationality, The Enemy Within*,
Constable, London, 1992.
I read this when my own text was near completion but I wish
I'd seen it earlier. Get this one, and keep it by you.

Accent

Honey, John, *Does Accent Matter?*, Faber and Faber, London,
1991.
If you're interested in what research shows about the effects of
different accents, this is the book.

Dress

Spillane, Mary, *Presenting Yourself: A personal image guide
for men*, Piatkus, 1993.
Spillane, Mary, *Presenting Yourself: A personal image guide
for women*, Piatkus, 1993.

Job Interviews

Fletcher, Clive, *Get that Job!*, Thorsons, London, 1986.
A useful practical guide, but it's worth looking around in a
good bookshop and choosing what suits you.
Leeds, Dorothy, *Secrets of Successful Interviews*, Piatkus, 1993.

Negotiating

Godefroy, Christian H. and Nierenberg, Gerard I., *The Art of
Negotiating*, Simon & Schuster, New York, 1986.
A best selling book with an American slant. A good text for the
top negotiator.
Scott, Bill, *The Skills of Negotiating*, Gower Press, Aldershot,
1981.
A less ambitious book than Nierenberg's, but I found it more
helpful for handling ordinary business negotiations.

Non Verbal Communication

Argyle, Michael, *Bodily Communication*, Methuen, London, 1975.
This is a comprehensive text for the serious student of NVC; but very accessible.
Nierenberg, Gerard I., and Calero, Henry H., *How to Read a Person Like a Book*, Heinrich Hanau, London, 1973.
The best practical book I know for anyone starting to look at NVC for the first time. Good line drawings.

Relaxing

Benson, Herbert, *The Relaxation Response*, Fount Paperbacks, London, 1977.
Martin, Ian C., *The Art and Practice of Relaxation*, Teach Yourself Books, London, 1978.
These are books I found helpful, but it's worth looking around in a good bookshop and choosing what suits you.

Consumer information

Consumers' Association Limited, 2 Marylebone Road, London NW1 4DF (This incorporates the 'Which? Personal Service' providing legal assistance for consumers.)
Australian Consumers' Association, 57 Carrington Road, Marrickville, NSW 2204, AUSTRALIA
Consumers' Association of Canada, Box 9300, Ottawa, Ontario K1G 3T9, CANADA
Consumer Council, Tower 6, 19th Floor, 33 Canton Road, Tsimshatsui, Kowloon, HONG KONG
Consumer Protection Association, PN Institute of Medical Sciences Campus, 'Jai Somnath', Himmat Nagar-383001, INDIA
Consumers' Association of Ireland, 45 Upper Mount Street, Dublin 2, IRELAND
Pahang Association of Consumers (PAC), Peti Surat No. 273, Kuantan, Pahang, MALAYSIA

Consumers' Association of New Zealand Inc., Private Bag, Te Aro, Wellington 6035, NEW ZEALAND

Church-Based Consumers' Association, NCCP Ecumenical Center Building, 879 East Delos Santos Avenue, Quezon City, PHILIPPINES

Consumers' Association of Singapore, BP 3370, Dakar, SINGAPORE

South African Co-ordinatoring Consumer Council, PO Box 3800, Pretoria 0001, SOUTH AFRICA

Consumers Union of United States Inc, 101 Truman Avenue, Yonkers, New York 10703, USA

Index of programs

Piatkus Business Books

Piatkus Business Books have been created for people who need expert knowledge readily available in a clear and easy-to-follow format. All the books are written by specialists in their field. They will help you improve your skills quickly and effortlessly in the workplace and on a personal level.
Titles include:

General Management and Business Skills

Beware the Naked Man Who Offers You His Shirt *Harvey Mackay*

Be Your Own PR Expert: the complete guide to publicity and public relations *Bill Penn*

Complete Conference Organiser's Handbook, The *Robin O'Connor*

Complete Time Management System, The *Christian H Godefroy and John Clark*

Confident Decision Making *J Edward Russo and Paul J H Schoemaker*

Energy Factor, The: how to motivate your workforce *Art McNeil*

Firing On All Cylinders: the quality management system for high-powered corporate performance *Jim Clemmer with Barry Sheehy*

How to Collect the Money You Are Owed *Malcolm Bird*

How to Implement Corporate Change *John Spencer and Adrian Pruss*

Influential Manager, The: how to develop a powerful management style *Lee Bryce*

Leadership Skills for Every Manager *Jim Clemmer and Art McNeil*

Lure the Tiger Out of the Mountains: timeless tactics from the East for today's successful manager *Gao Yuan*

Managing Your Team *John Spencer and Adrian Pruss*

Winning Edge, The *Charles Templeton*

Self-Improvement

Brain Power: the 12-week mental training programme
  Marilyn vos Savant and Leonore Fleischer
Creating Abundance *Andrew Ferguson*
Creative Thinking *Michael LeBoeuf*
Memory Booster: easy techniques for rapid learning and a
  better memory *Robert W Finkel*
Organise Yourself *Ronni Eisenberg with Kate Kelly*
Quantum Learning: unleash the genius within you *Bobbi*
  DePorter with Mike Hernacki
Right Brain Manager, The: how to use the power of your
  mind to achieve personal and professional success *Dr*
  Harry Alder
Three Minute Meditator, The *David Harp with Nina*
  Feldman

Sales and Customer Services

Art of the Hard Sell, The *Robert L Shook*
Creating Customers *David H Bangs*
Guerrilla Marketing Excellence *Jay Conrad Levinson*
How to Close Every Sale *Joe Girard*
How to Make Your Fortune Through Network Marketing
  John Bremner
How to Succeed in Network Marketing *Leonard Hawkins*
How to Win Customers and Keep Them for Life *Michael*
  LeBoeuf
How to Write Letters that Sell *by Christian Godefroy*
Sales Power: the Silva mind method for sales professionals
  Jose Silva and Ed Bernd Jr
Selling Edge, The *Patrick Forsyth*
Telephone Selling Techniques That Really Work *Bill*
  Good
Winning New Business: a practical guide to successful
  sales presentations *Dr David Lewis*

Presentation and Communication

Better Business Writing *Maryann V Piotrowski*

Complete Book of Business Etiquette, The *Lynne Brennan and David Block*

Confident Conversation *Dr Lillian Glass*

Confident Speaking: how to communicate effectively using the Power Talk System *Christian H Godefroy and Stephanie Barrat*

He Says, She Says: closing the communication gap between the sexes *Dr Lillian Glass*

Personal Power *Philippa Davies*

Powerspeak: the complete guide to public speaking and presentation *Dorothy Leeds*

Presenting Yourself: a personal image guide for men *Mary Spillane*

Presenting Yourself: a personal image guide for women *Mary Spillane*

Say What You Mean and Get What You Want *George R. Walther*

Your Total Image *Philippa Davies*

Careers and Training

How to Find the Perfect Job *Tom Jackson*

Marketing Yourself: how to sell yourself and get the jobs you've always wanted *Dorothy Leeds*

Networking and Mentoring: a women's guide *Dr Lily M Segerman-Peck*

Perfect CV, The *Tom Jackson*

Perfect Job Search Strategies *Tom Jackson*

Secrets of Successful Interviews *Dorothy Leeds*

Sharkproof: get the job you want, keep the job you love in today's tough job market *Harvey Mackay*

10-Day MBA, The *Steven Silbiger*

Ten Steps To The Top *Marie Jennings*

Which Way Now? – how to plan and develop a successful career *Bridget Wright*

For a free brochure with further information on our complete range of business titles, please write to:
Piatkus Books
Freepost 7 (WD 4505)
London W1E 4EZ

PIATKUS